Graham Rice

GROW VEGETABLES, FRUIT, HERBS AND FLOWERS IN THE SAME SPACE

all-in-one garden

CASSELL ILLUSTRATED

First published in Great Britain in 2006 by Cassell Illustrated
a division of Octopus Publishing Group Limited
2–4 Heron Quays, London E14 4JP

Distributed in the United States of America by
Sterling Publishing Co., Inc.,
387 Park Avenue South, New York, NY 10016-8810

A CIP catalogue record for this book is available from the British Library.

ISBN-13: 978-1-844034-51-2
ISBN-10: 1-844034-51-8

10 9 8 7 6 5 4 3 2 1

Designed by Nigel Soper

Printed in China

Contents

Introduction

Vegetables, fruit and herbs are no longer just food and flavouring. They are much more than that. As new varieties of food plants have been introduced, which are more productive, more resistant to pests and diseases and – yes – perhaps even tastier, they have also become more attractive to look at, vegetables in particular. Many edible plants have risen so much in their ability to serve as invaluable ornamentals – and then be served at table – that they deserve to be liberated from the veg patch to join the petunias and poppies, the hostas and heucheras in the wider world of the all-in-one garden.

The elegance and attractiveness of these vegetables and herbs provide a wonderful opportunity. Lettuces are not just round and green, now they are frilly or oak-leaved and come in a wide range of shades, from red tinted to deep crimson. Chards have broken out of their traditional dullness and are now available in a veritable rainbow of colours. The bright flower colours and bicolours of runner beans justify their use as ornamental climbers – and, of course, there are the beans to follow. Many herbs also come in an increasing range of decorative foliage and flowering variants, such as the huge choices of mints, sages and other herbs that come in variegated or golden-leaved varieties.

With so many edible plants worth growing for their visual appeal there is no longer any excuse for not including them in your garden. There is no reason to say 'I do not have the space', and no need to hide vegetables away in a separate plot behind a hedge.

Back in the 1970s there was astonishment – not to say consternation – when visitors to the Royal Botanic Gardens at Kew found that the beds in front of the Palm House, the summer showcase for the gardens, were planted with potatoes and ruby chard, lettuce and parsley. But it proved a triumph, and an eye-opener for visitors from all over the world (not to mention garden students like me).

Against a background of mixed chards, garlic chives with their flat white flower heads and mild garlic flavour stand out and are fronted by a planting of purple kale.

Since then, wherever I've gardened, I've blended food plants and flowers. From marigolds and curly parsley in a hanging basket on the little balcony of my first flat and canary creeper climbing up the tomatoes, to later planning and planting of more expansive schemes and growing clematis up into mature apple trees.

In recent years, I've been especially interested in bringing flowers and food plants together into all-in-one seasonal plantings. Summer flowers like ageratum, verbena, petunias, salpiglossis, morning glories, and salvias – all in blue and white – interplanted with black Tuscan kale, purple curly kale and leeks was especially successful. A red and white version also worked very well and featured bedding geraniums, salvias, verbena, dahlias and coleus with beetroot, red lettuce and nasturtiums. And all these can be reduced down in scale to the level of a single container if you have space for nothing more.

Here I learned a hard lesson: in containers of all kinds, watering is absolutely crucial. If containers dry out and the plants wilt they're never quite the same again. Skipping the watering in the rush to get out and enjoy a summer day can ruin both the crop and the display for the whole season. Fortunately, water-retentive container composts, an outside tap and a drip watering system can simplify watering all-in-one containers enormously – and believe me, it's worth it. And regular watering pays off in beds and borders too.

There are now so many varieties of fruit and vegetables that are worth growing because they look good enough to more than justify a place in beds, borders and containers alongside perennials, shrubs and annuals, providing both colour and food. This means that even in the smallest spaces you can grow food plants and enhance the beauty of your garden.

Fiery California poppies, with their dissected silvery foliage, self sow amongst the purple cabbages and keep coming back year after year.

01 | Food and Flowers

'Don't try to tell me that a cabbage is as beautiful as a rose,' you are saying. Well, maybe I am not … maybe. But what I am saying is that a vast range of productive and easy-to-grow fruit, vegetables and herbs are well worth growing for their ornamental qualities as well as for their flavour. Flowers, fruits, fragrance, foliage colour, shape, texture, habit and woody structure are all features that food plants can provide if you choose the right ones. It is also partly a matter of mindset, of how you think about plants. If you banish your preconceptions and think about fruit, vegetables and herbs as ornamentals, like hostas or petunias, rather than as utilitarian food plants, it is then easier to consider them as you plan your borders.

Some beans would be worth growing for their flowers even if they never produced food. Meanwhile, sparkling blossom could be followed by a tree dripping with crab apples, a warming autumn sight, and they make lovely aromatic jelly. Many lettuces, kales and cabbages form bold and colourful foliage plants. There are plenty of options when painting with edible plants, such as using the vivid green and tightly curled texture of parsley, the architectural stature of angelica and the winter outline of a fan-trained fruit tree on a wall.

Train runner beans up an apple tree or interplant the parsley with French marigolds and you create delightful plant pictures, which are not only attractive in their own right but also provide you with food and flavouring. What a treat!

Overwintered curly kales stretch upwards before they open their yellow flowers and make imposing plants amongst dahlias, gazanias and other summer flowers.

The attraction of fresh food

Taste and goodness

There is no doubt about it, fresh food is good for you – and the fresher the better. For example, nutrient-rich kale, which is one of the most attractive of vegetables in the all-in-one garden, loses up to 5 per cent of its vitamin C content in each hour after cutting. Three-quarters of its most important nutrient could be lost before it even reaches the supermarket. So if you can take it from your garden to the steamer in a matter of minutes and then on to your family's plates you will be rewarded by their, and your, good health.

In addition, the moment vegetables are cut, chemical changes start to take place that reduce their characteristic natural flavours so that when you eat 'fresh' vegetables from the supermarket their taste may well disappoint you.

Fresh produce looks better too. Have you ever reached for the pencil beans or the chards in the supermarket and then drawn back and moved on when you see how wilted they are? Salad vegetables are 95 per cent water, and it takes only a 2 per cent loss of moisture for them to start to wilt. But they are so delicious when eaten fresh from the garden.

There is one other thing. Most fresh vegetables, fruits and herbs from the supermarket or farmers' market are treated with chemicals to kill or prevent pest, disease or weed problems. Sadly, even some produce labelled 'organic' turns out to contain traces of pesticides. In recent years many of the most harmful chemicals have been withdrawn, but the problem with any shop-bought produce is that you can never know for sure what treatments it has received. At least in your own garden you know exactly how your food has been grown. If you choose not to spray, you can be sure your food has not been sprayed. If you do spray, you can decide for yourself precisely which treatments to use.

Family life

How do your kids find out that potatoes do not grow on trees? From the drawings on a school handout? From a field trip where they are so pleased not to be in class that they do not really pay attention? Well, they could find out at home, every day, in your own garden.

My mother had the right idea but the wrong plan. She gave me some radish seeds to plant when I was a kid. I was delighted when they emerged through the soil in just a few days. In a month they were ready to pull. I had actually grown some food myself, and it was ready before I was bored by the whole idea. The trouble was that when I tasted my very first home-grown radish I spat it out and with it went any interest in gardening, or where food came from, for more than a decade.

OK, so forget radishes for enticing kids. Instead, grow apples, mint, lettuces and potatoes alongside the flowers in your garden and have your kids around while you are sowing seeds and planting trees. If you have them help with planting and picking as just another part of family life, an understanding of where food comes from will seep into them without it

The all-in-one garden can provide plenty of fresh tasty produce while at the same time making a valuable contribution to an attractive garden display.

becoming a school lesson at home. And it can all happen naturally in an arena that is not just row after row of the same old plants. Children will want to be in a garden that looks and smells wonderful, and you will not have to drag them down to the allotment or to the corner of the garden that looks more boring than everywhere else. They will have watched it grow, and even the fussiest will be more inclined to eat it.

There is also entertainment value in a garden where flowers and ornamental food plants mingle attractively. When guests come for dinner you can all go round the garden enjoying the flowers and fragrances and picking leaves so that in the course of a relaxed conversation in lovely surroundings you have gathered the ingredients for a salad. Pick rosemary from a sunny border and use it with lamb cutlets on the grill; snip the dill to go with your fish.

Your all-in-one garden can be part of your kids' life, your family life and your social life if it blends flowers and food in an attractive way.

Graham's top child-friendly crops

- Carrots
- Mint
- Pumpkins
- Strawberries

Being able to watch food crops grow and taste them straight from the plant gives children a greater understanding of where food comes from and can help to foster a life-long enjoyment of gardening.

Growing food in small spaces

Food with flowers

Integrating foods and flowers into an all-in-one garden is the way to make small gardens not only good to look at but also a wonderful source of nourishment. In small areas, setting aside a specific area to grow food is almost impossible without disrupting the whole design of the garden. And although some veg fanatics will happily look out of their windows at traditional long rows of turnips and onions side by side, gardens that must look good to the whole family – not to mention friends and neighbours – need another approach.

The planting areas in most modern small gardens are either designed as mixed plantings or develop that way. A tree or two, shrubs, climbers on the fence and on wigwams of canes, perennials, bulbs and annuals intermingle into a year-round display. Add ornamental forms of vegetables, herbs and fruit and your borders will look just as good but will be edible too! There are mixed-planting ideas that can be incorporated in every part of the garden.

That flowering cherry tree may look stunning for only two weeks of the whole year, yet at other times it can support yellow-leaved runner beans with a carpet of ground-covering strawberries below. Or you could make the most of an eating apple tree, with its flowers in spring and fruits in autumn, by training a clematis into it to provide colour in between. And when you need evergreens for winter interest, think about rosemary with winter iris alongside.

Perhaps you need hardy perennials for your border? If so, cardoons are superb in front of blue delphiniums and will rise up to take their place later in summer when the delphiniums are over. Pink-flowered chives are the most adaptable of perennials and look great alongside silvery leaved heucheras or dead nettles. And when it comes to annuals, for beds or containers, a carpet of blue and white petunias under blue-black Tuscan kale make an impressive summer-long picture – even after you have picked some of the kale for the kitchen.

Graham's all-in-one planting ideas

- Curly parsley makes a superb foliage plant for containers and sets off flowers beautifully.
- Train red- and white-flowered runner beans, instead of sweet peas, up a wigwam of canes.
- Use one of the coloured-leaved varieties of sage (golden, purple or variegated) for a front-of-the-border evergreen shrub.

On their own – but looking good

Although the best way to achieve a genuinely all-in-one garden is to mingle ornamental food plants with more familiar ornamentals, if you have the space or the desire to go a step further it is possible to create attractive, productive and tasty plantings made up solely of ornamental food plants. The look can be enhanced by breaking away from the traditional planting scheme of long rows, which usually produce far too much produce for a family anyway. Instead, plant in raised beds supported by elegant, perhaps coloured, boards or organize the planting in a potager – a more or less formal design of small beds in which individual varieties are planted in different sections (*see* pages 52–56 for further information on raised beds).

For example, a bed 0.9–1.2m (3–4ft) wide can be raised between vertical boards 15–20cm (6–8in) wide and then planted in short rows. Red lettuces, slender spring onions, feathery carrots, purple-leaved beets and more can be planted alongside each other to create an ever-changing succession of colour and produce. If the boards are stained with one of the vast variety of safe coloured preservatives now available, and gravel or bark used for the path alongside, the result can be spectacular.

Another approach is to grow annual vegetables and herbs instead of annual flowers and bedding plants for summer. So try purple-leaved curly kale with red-flowered dwarf runner beans, yellow-leaved feverfew and purple-leaved beet. So many attractive, sun-loving herbs can be grown together that creating an unattractive herb garden is almost impossible.

Even a single container can be planted with blueberries – attractive in three different seasons – or with trailing tomatoes and purple basil, which look great together on the patio and complement each other in the kitchen.

Graham's sun-loving ornamental herbs

- BASIL Rich purple or green foliage, including miniature forms, and spikes of dainty blue or white flowers.
- OREGANO White-edged foliage with an especially fresh, aromatic appeal.
- ROSEMARY Flowers in blue or pink, or with yellow-splashed leaves.
- SAGE Purple or yellow-edged or multicoloured leaves and with blue, pink or white flowers.
- THYME Creeping or bushy, with ruby to white flowers and green or variegated leaves.

Ornamental forms of herbs like this purple sage and golden tansy are vital ingredients of the all-in-one garden, adding colour, flavour and fragrance.

The broad, fresh green foliage of dwarf beans looks well when grown with feathery-leaved carrots and the divided, bronze-purple foliage of dahlias.

Initial planning

There is, of course, a difference between beginning a brand-new garden, which is an empty canvas, and adapting the style of an existing garden to accommodate food plants. In a new garden you will be choosing everything. So you can plant one of the slender, upright eating apples – with spring flowers, fruits later and a bold and distinctive winter structure – instead of a relatively unproductive birch as your ornamental tree. Remember to think outside the box when it comes to planting choices.

You can position thornless blackberries on the fence instead of a clematis – more now have attractive flowers and foliage as well as scrumptious fruit.

Choose blueberries for your permanent containers and, when it comes to perennials, artichokes (globe and Jerusalem), golden tansy and rhubarb (which is sensational in flower). Annual vegetables are also assets, and a good range of foliage forms in particular is now available.

When taking over existing plantings the first thing to do is assess what you have – and ruthlessly remove anything that is sickly or that you simply dislike. Good plants can also be restricted if they have grown too big. This immediately provides openings for attractive vegetables, fruits and herbs to be slipped in.

Annual vegetables and herbs, as well as fruit, can quickly make a difference both to the look of the garden and to the flavour of your food. Just as a start, in any situation that is not hot and sunny, yellow-leaved 'Golden Alexandra' alpine strawberries, with their sweet and tasty little berries, can be raised from seed or bought as plants. They can readily be slotted into vacant spaces.

Graham's top food plants for an existing garden

- PARSLEY Curly parsley goes with just about every other low-growing plant in the garden and is also great in containers.
- RUNNER BEANS Dwarf, red- and white-flowered runners flower all summer if the beans are picked regularly.
- STRAWBERRIES Regular fruiting strawberries as groundcover and yellow-leaved alpine strawberries to brighten up the shade.

Choosing crops wisely

The three qualities to seek when selecting vegetables, fruits and herbs for the all-in-one garden are visual appeal, flavour and yield. Look for a balance of all three, because varieties that look wonderful, crop well yet taste of nothing really do not do the job – you might as well plant petunias. These three qualities, together with resistance to pests and diseases, ease of culture and size of crop relative to the area occupied, should guide decisions on what to plant.

LEFT: *Black Tuscan kale is a striking, long-lasting food and foliage plant that makes a distinctive shape in the border and a tasty vegetable if steamed gently.*

Sometimes it may be a matter of choosing the right crop: few would say that turnips have much visual appeal, so they are never going to replace hostas as ornamentals. On the other hand, all runner beans look attractive in flower. Vegetables such as turnips, swedes, radishes, parsnips, celery and cauliflowers really have little place in the all-in-one garden; nor do horseradish and some mints, as they can be rampantly invasive. Yet there are numerous invaluable food plants that are also decorative. Most tomatoes and peppers look great; carrot foliage is always attractive; all varieties of Swiss chard, sage, thyme, rosemary and fennel are appealing; and apples have

RIGHT: *Runner beans would be worth growing for their scarlet flowers even if they never produced any crop. They are at their most colourful before they develop too many leaves.*

three seasons of interest. Figs always look good even if they never bear fruit!

Sometimes, you need to be a little discerning. The varieties of some crops have such diverse characteristics that it is important to select carefully. The red- and purple-leaved varieties of cabbages and Brussels sprouts are more useful than the plain green ones. Some varieties of early potato flower prolifically, while others are much more sparse. Curly parsley looks better than flat-leaved parsley. Many lettuces are attractive, and some varieties go to seed quickly, although red-leaved variants are eye-catching as they do so. Some variegated mints look superb and these are less invasive. It is easy to pick the especially attractive varieties of bush beans, beetroot, basil, peas, pumpkins and squashes and the rest, so your final planting decision will often be based simply on colour.

Graham's top ten all-in-one garden crops
- Blueberries (for containers)
- Chards
- Coloured-leaved sage
- Curly parsley
- Purple curly kale
- Red and curly lettuce
- Red cabbage
- Runner beans
- Strawberries
- Variegated mints

colour, big on cropping

Long season crops

With many traditional crops, you pick them once they are ready and then they are gone – end of story. In small gardens and especially in the all-in-one garden this is simply not good enough. What you need is this: a crop that is attractive while it is developing; looks good when it is ripe; stays ready and appealing for longer… and longer; and then, preferably, can be partially picked, leaving the rest still looking great. Plants should also integrate well with surrounding ornamentals.

Some perennial candidates, like many ornamental herbs, are attractive from when they emerge from the ground in spring right through to autumn – variegated mints are a prime example. Some, like sage and rosemary, are evergreen and can provide 12 months of colour and cropping. Perennial vegetables such as rhubarb, seakale and globe artichokes are decorative enough to grow even if they were not edible.

Some seasonal plants are a great deal more persistent than others. Cabbages, kales, Brussels sprouts, leeks, chards and some carrots give many months of colour and interest. Fruits like crab apples, blackberries and blueberries provide different appeals at different seasons – flowers, fruits and foliage – while golden hop has its buttery foliage colour for months on end.

This new way of thinking may require a fresh view of familiar vegetables. And while many gardeners are looking back to the flavour of heritage varieties, often the new introductions have the best staying power both in terms of colour and cropping.

Graham's top crops for long season interest
- Blueberries
- Chards
- Crab apples
- Globe artichokes
- Golden hops
- Kales
- Red cabbages
- Rhubarb
- Rosemary
- Sages

LEFT: *Both ornamental and edible foliage plants, such as cannas, coleus, cabbage and kale create a long lasting attraction in a sunny border.*

RIGHT: *These ornamental kales are as colourful as the marigolds, nasturtiums and California poppies around them in this summer and autumn combination.*

The long harvest

Not only have plant breeders created varieties that look good for longer, but they have also listened to gardeners' needs for varieties that do not crop in a rush and then spoil – that is, varieties that hold their quality over a long period. Thus they have exactly met the requirements of the all-in-one gardener.

A long season is invaluable, because in many cases the plants are removed once the harvest is complete and you are left with, well, nothing. So crops that last are inherently useful. Vegetables that create an especially long presence in the garden include sprouts, cabbages, looseleaf lettuce, climbing beans and courgettes; among herbs, parsley and all the naturally perennial types, such as mint and sage, also have a long season of impact.

In many cases, choosing the right type or the right variety of a plant is very important, and here again recent introductions can be especially useful. Modern lettuces stand well without running to seed far better than most old-fashioned varieties. New carrot varieties, which can be picked when they are small and juicy or left to mature into long, fat roots, provide that vital combination of cropping opportunities and foliage interest for far longer than those that split and rot if they are not pulled small. Modern chards hold well, because when you snap off some leaves for cooking more foliage keeps appearing.

Breeding is all done using traditional techniques, I might say; there are no genetically modified varieties in garden vegetables and fruits. Vegetable breeders have also paid attention to the cries of 'give us more flavour' and done exactly that. Because the older heritage varieties often have a fine flavour but comparatively poor yields, there was a period when only higher yields were trumpeted as new varieties appeared. Now flavour, texture and a long harvest season are emphasized as well as yield. Combine these characteristics with better pest and disease resistance (so you need to bother less about whether or not to spray) and more tolerance of drought and other climatic extremes, as well as a wider colour range, and it is clear that modern fruit, vegetable and herb varieties are invaluable to the all-in-one gardener.

Graham's top ten long harvest crops
- Cabbages
- Chards
- Climbing beans
- Courgettes
- Lettuces
- Mints
- Oregano
- Parsley
- Sages
- Sprouts

Even green is a useful colour
Edible plants do not need to be red or variegated in order to be attractive. Green is a worthwhile colour, too. After all, our gardens are full of wonderful green-leaved hostas so what is wrong with green vegetables?

Of course, the green foliage of some vegetables is singularly unremarkable – no one would plant a turnip for the look of its leaves, but in terms of form, texture and colour many green-leaved vegetables are well worth growing, and they integrate especially well with the widest range of flowers.

For broad foliage cabbages, sprouts, beetroot, some lettuces, chards, courgettes and their relations, some kales and rhubarb are excellent. The deeply lobed foliage of oak-leaf lettuces, figs and angelica and the more jagged leaves of globe artichokes and cardoons

These striking, purple-tinted leeks are surrounded by a row of curly parsley and a permanent edging of chives to create an attractive formal planting.

are very attractive, as is the deeply feathered foliage of dill and fennel, carrots, chamomile and 'leafless' peas. The slender leaves of onions, leeks, garlic chives and chives make a bold contrast in a bed of broader foliage.

Curly kale and curly parsley are supreme among foliage food plants, while many herbs, like oregano, mint and rosemary, also have attractive green leaves – as do strawberries, which make excellent groundcover. Once you look at these plants with the dispassionate eye of a designer wishing to create striking plant combinations, these additions to your palette of colours, shapes and textures develop a new life as ornamentals and their leaf qualities become apparent.

Graham's top ten green-leaved food plants
- Carrots
- Chives
- Fennel
- Figs
- Kales
- Lettuces
- Parsley
- Pumpkin and squash family
- Rosemary
- Strawberries

Short rows of crops suit a small garden and a small family, and this edging of colourful marigolds makes an attractive feature.

Cut-and-come-again salads

Cut-and-come-again (CCA) salads are those sown in a carpet and snipped off when a few centimetres high and which then resprout. They come into their own in spring. In a block in a raised bed or in a trough on the patio, balcony or deck the prettiest pictures – both in the garden and in the salad bowl – come from seed mixtures containing a range of different salad plants. These are sold under names like Mixed Lettuce Leaves, Mixed Salad Leaves, Saladini, Saladisi™ and Mesclun Mix. Besides the freshness of their youth, these salad mixes combine a range of colours and forms for a splendid groundcover around a taller plant.

Chinese mustards make excellent CCA crops. After these are cut they will re-grow to provide a second crop from the same space.

If you spread CCA plants in small areas throughout the all-in-one garden, you can cut them without making obvious holes in the planting design, and they will also create echoes of desirable harmonies within the garden.

CCA salads are very easy to grow (*see* page 116). Start with one of the special seed mixtures from the garden centre or a mail order catalogue, although you may want to try a number of different mixes in just one season, because these crops are ready so quickly.

Some gardeners simply decide on the area they wish to cover, rake it to a fine crumbly texture, scatter the seed thinly and rake again. This works but it makes identifying weed seedlings difficult and when you have cut part of a large patch it looks a little silly. It is therefore better to sow the seeds in individual rows just as you would any other vegetable. If the effect you need is of a narrow band snaking through a border or making a neat temporary pattern, simply draw the drill where you will. If you need a wider band, make two rows 5cm (2in) apart (this will allow you to remove weeds from between the rows) or use a hoe to make a flat-bottomed sowing area 10cm (4in) across and scatter the seed there. Three or four rows can go along the length of a 23cm (9in) wide trough.

Raising your own or buying in

The way in which you start growing your plants is an important factor when it comes to ensuring good colour and good cropping over a long season, and it particularly affects seed-raised plants, which includes most vegetables. However, with fruits, perennial vegetables and herbs, which grow in the same place for at least a few years, this is less of an issue as plants are widely available in garden centres or by mail order.

Traditionally, vegetable seeds were simply sown in a row. The resulting seedlings were thinned out to allow them more space, then thinned again to their final spacings, which they then grew to fill. The problem with this for the all-in-one gardener is that for many weeks the most obvious feature of the area where the plants are growing is bare soil. And, frankly, bare soil is exactly what you are trying to avoid. There are two ways of making sure that as little bare soil as possible is on view: sowing and transplanting, and buying in plants.

Sowing and transplanting involves raising plants from seed sown in pots or in seed or plug trays in a bright but sheltered corner of the garden or in a cold frame, unheated or heated greenhouse or a porch (*see* page 164). Seedlings in pots and trays are moved into individual pots and grown on to a size where they will make an impact as soon as they are planted; those sown in plug trays may be thinned or left in clusters and grown on to planting size without transplanting. A similar approach can be applied to perennial herbs and other plants raised by cuttings or division, by bringing on the young plants in pots.

It is also now possible to buy an increasing range of vegetable plants (from tomatoes to leeks) by mail order, usually from seed companies, and these can either go straight into the garden or be grown to a larger size for a few weeks in pots before planting.

These plants – whether raised at home or bought in – have especial value when you need to keep the all-in-one garden looking good. As a crop loses its appeal in the kitchen and in the garden it can be replaced by a plant that makes an immediate impact.

Graham's top five easy-to-raise crops
- Beans (bush and climbing)
- Brussels sprouts
- Cut-and-come-again salads
- Kales
- Lettuces

RIGHT: *Seedlings of courgettes and other members of the pumpkin family can be raised in pots in a warm place and then planted out when the danger of frost is past.*

02 | Sites and Situations

Growing food and flowers together is not an approach that requires special conditions or particular situations – you can try it anywhere. On balconies, bushy herbs like sage can be grown in containers with trailing hardy geraniums, and window-boxes can be planted with parsley and impatiens. Tall, upright tomatoes can be cultivated in containers with morning glory, while trailing tomatoes can go in hanging baskets with lobelia. Rosemary and other Mediterranean herbs just love sunny raised beds with dainty wild crocuses and irises.

In small beds and borders there is a host of choices, including the use of coloured, leafy chards with verbena or bronze-leaved shrubs. On a larger scale, red cabbages and sprouts make an almost tropical display with phormiums and castor oil plants.

This joyful jumble of food and flowers has been augmented by adding a container of annuals in colours that harmonise with the surrounding plants.

Strawberries provide good groundcover in shade, while in sun, even in hot, dry conditions, many herbs are at their most aromatic. Nowhere – absolutely nowhere in the garden in which plants will grow – need be excluded from the all-in-one garden approach.

Small borders

Small in scale, big on harvest

Having a small garden or only a small area of it in which to try the all-in-one approach this should not stop you creating attractive flower and food combinations to provide both colour and culinary ingredients. The trick is to choose crops that will give you the largest, tastiest food from your small site. Therefore, big and bushy plants with a low yield, like peas and globe artichokes, should be left out of small borders in favour of more productive crops that occupy less space.

Utilizing vertical space is crucial. Cane fruits, grapes or fan-trained tree fruits, or even runner beans, can be grown on fences. To provide support, tie them to three or four horizontal strands of galvanized wire attached to the fence 45–60cm (18–24in) apart. You should also make the most of the sides of the house, garage, shed or summerhouse as plant supports, and of garden walls, by attaching trellis or wires. In the border itself, using vertical space is again important – even if you have to create it yourself.

A single stout post – 2.4m (8ft) high, knocked in 45–60cm (18–24in) deep – can be used as support for a raspberry plant, which provides white flowers in spring and drips with berries in summer. Or attach a vertical cylinder of 2.5cm (1in) mesh galvanized wire to the post and you have a support for climbing beans.

Now that dwarf and columnar fruit trees are available, often grafted on to rootstocks that ensure they stay small, fruit can be introduced as a focal point into small borders, with other planting below it. Cherries, apples, crab apples – even peaches and nectarines in sheltered areas with hot summers – can make attractive specimens with early flowers, fruit later and perhaps autumn colour. But in a small space be sure not to create too much shade.

All these verticals can be enhanced by planting annual climbers, like annual convolvulus or canary creeper, to scramble through them for the summer, together with a wide range of perennials below.

Graham's top ten croppers for small spaces

- Bushy evergreen herbs
  (such as rosemary, sage)
- Cut-and-come-again crops
- Chards
- Chives
- Climbing and bushy French beans
- Climbing and bushy runner beans
- Looseleaf lettuces
- Mizuna greens
- Parsley
- Tayberries

Intimate portraits

In small spaces plants naturally grow closely together, and this provides opportunities to create decorative plant pictures on a diminutive scale. Sometimes there

This permanent planting of fruit and flowers features a standard apple tree underplanted with hostas and a contrasting clipped bun of box.

can be a fine distinction between plants growing intimately and one plant overwhelming its neighbour, and in a small space particularly it takes a little time and careful attention to maintain a good balance.

Tomatoes are often among the first plants that gardeners integrate into flower borders. They are widely available in a range of varieties; the fruits come in red, yellow and even striped and purple versions, as well as in many shapes and sizes; and they are easy to grow. There are two types – tall tomatoes and bush tomatoes – and both are useful.

Plant a tall tomato in sun and train it against a stout, preferably green, stake. Water and feed it, and it will grow well. The small, yellowish, green flowers are followed by green fruits, which ripen to yellow or red. Cherry-fruited tomatoes produce the most attractive display and will yield the best crop over a long period during the growing season.

Yellow canary creeper can be planted to twine prettily among the scarlet tomatoes, while dwarf white cosmos will hide basal stems and also make a good neighbour; plant it at the same time as the tomatoes and immediately pinch out the tips to encourage bushy plants. The fine foliage and long season of colourful cosmos daisies look lovely alongside the bolder tomato foliage and bright fruits. Clouds of flowers from dwarf perennial gypsophila also make good companions, and blue campanulas, such as 'Kent Belle', could rest their stems on the tomatoes from nearby.

The bare stems of the maturing red tomatoes are masked at the base by bushy zinnias in the same shade of red as the rapidly ripening fruits.

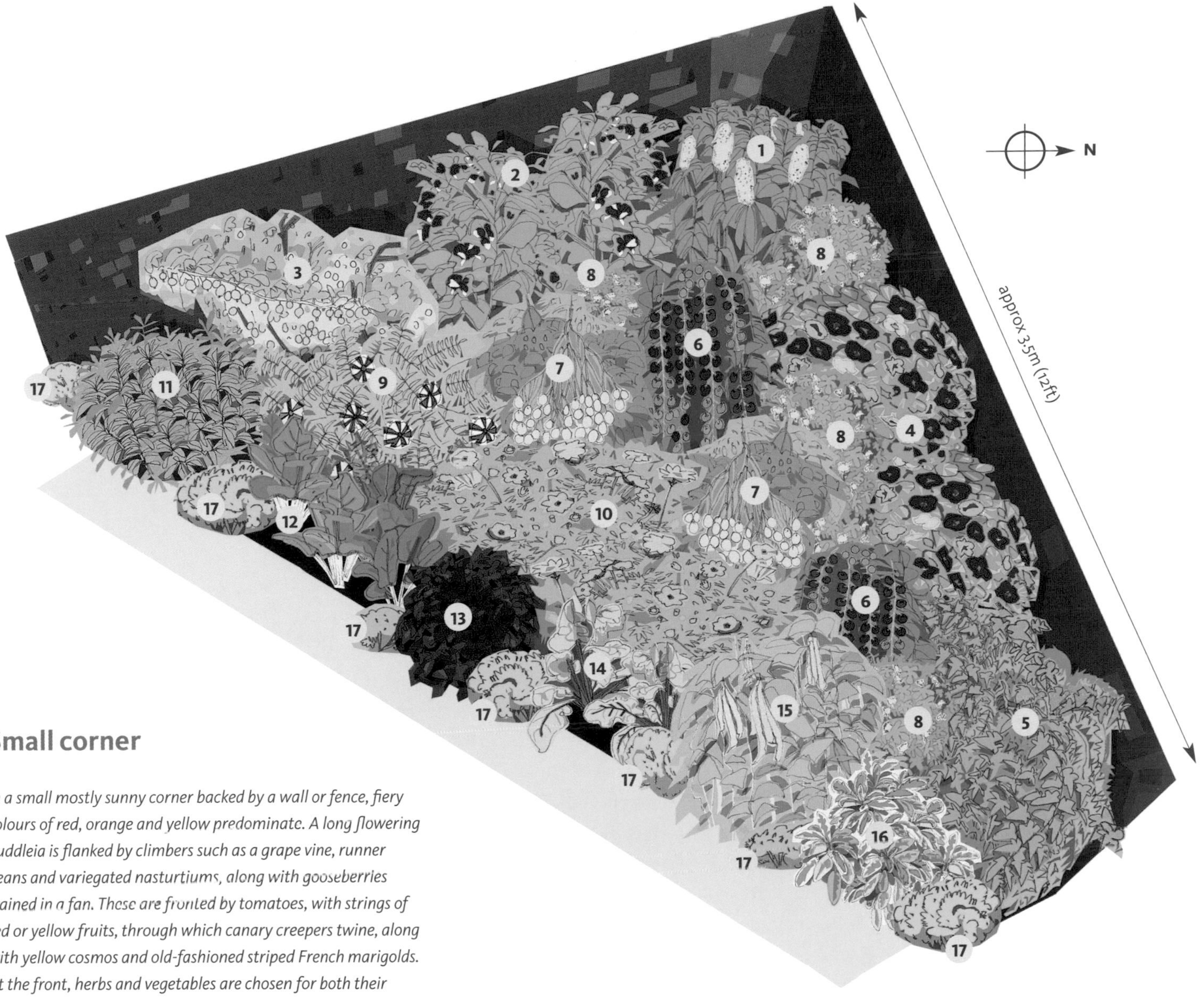

approx 3.5m (12ft)

N

Small corner

In a small mostly sunny corner backed by a wall or fence, fiery colours of red, orange and yellow predominate. A long flowering buddleia is flanked by climbers such as a grape vine, runner beans and variegated nasturtiums, along with gooseberries trained in a fan. These are fronted by tomatoes, with strings of red or yellow fruits, through which canary creepers twine, along with yellow cosmos and old-fashioned striped French marigolds. At the front, herbs and vegetables are chosen for both their culinary and ornamental qualities and include sage, lettuce, chard and beans in striking shades interplanted with invaluable curly parsley.

1 Buddleia 'Sungold'
2 Runner bean 'Painted Lady'
3 Gooseberry
4 Variegated nasturtium *Tropaeolum* 'Jewel of Africa'
5 Vine

6 Tomato 'Sweet 100'
7 Tomato 'Ildi'
8 Canary creeper
9 Marigold 'Harlequin'
10 *Cosmos sulphurous* 'Polidor'
11 Purple sage

12 Chard 'Bright Yellow'
13 Red lettuce 'Red Salad Bowl'
14 Ruby chard 'Rhubarb Chard'
15 Yellow beans 'Golden Teepee'
16 Sage 'Icterina'
17 Parsley 'Afro'

Bush tomatoes vary enormously in growth, but those intended for hanging baskets are sufficiently compact to go right at the front of a garden bed, especially if borders are edged with a vertical board or a raised stone. As they tumble over the edge, bushy trailing plants with loose rather than smothering growth can be placed alongside, so that they intermingle. Trailing lobelia, best in blue or white, can be planted at the same time as the tomatoes. Some perennials work well, too: for example, the red-centred, peachy flowers of *Potentilla* x *tonguei* will sneak among the tomatoes on questing stems from nearby, as will the silver-leaved, white-flowered dead nettle, *Lamium maculatum* 'White Nancy'. If either becomes overdominant and threatens to smother, it is easy to nip off the offending shoots.

Graham's top tips for intimate portraits

- Choose climbers that are appropriate to their support if you wish to train them on taller and more substantial plants as supports.
- Consider foliage forms and avoid competing and clashing colours.
- Encourage plants to intermingle freely and nestle naturally together.
- Utilize as many heights and levels as possible when creating your plant pictures by introducing bushy low plants to cover the bases of taller plants.

After the harvest

There comes a time when plants have yielded their crop and have to be removed. This may well leave a gap – but not necessarily. Your choice of varieties can assist here. If you choose looseleaf rather than hearting lettuce you can keep picking a few leaves for months, rather than have to cut the whole head in one go. Chards, kales and several oriental vegetables can also be harvested regularly.

Eventually, however, the crop will finish and you will have a space, which may in fact already have been 'filled'. One clever trick with seasonal vegetables is to plant them over bulbs, which stay in place permanently; daffodils are ideal although it is important to plant them deeply to avoid their being skewered with your trowel when you plant over them. The bulbs will emerge into clear soil or through what you have planted over them. Or you could plant basil over autumn crocuses, which will take over just as the basil is scorched by the first frost.

Another way to fill a planting gap is to have young replacements coming on or to buy young plants from the garden centre. In some cases the replacements may simply be a later sowing of what has just been removed: lettuce, for example, or other short-term leafy vegetables. In others, the new planting may take your cropping forward into another season: for example, leeks following a spring crop.

Alternatively, you can change tack and sow seed of quick-growing annuals, like linaria, Virginia stocks

A large, maturing, red-leaved lettuce allows a complementary planting of lobelia and flatleaf and curly parsley to fill the surrounding spaces.

or poached egg plant (*Limnanthes*), and slot food plants in to replace earlier annuals elsewhere as they fade.

Yet another option, when a short-term crop comes out, is to replace it with divisions of a perennial herb from elsewhere in the border. When they are established, the original can be removed and replaced by an entirely different plant.

Best of all, perhaps, is to plan the succession by interplanting late-flowering perennials, such as asters, with a summer crop, like looseleaf lettuce. By the time the lettuce is finished the aster will be filling the space and in the meantime will provide the lettuce plants with summer shade. In a small space, which enjoys close and constant scrutiny, change is good and as crops decline they provide just such an opportunity.

Graham's top tips for avoiding bare spots

- Buy young plants as replacements or have them ready in pots to take over as plants are removed.
- Make successional sowings of crops such as looseleaf lettuces.
- Plant over spring- and autumn-flowering bulbs.
- Plant quick-growing crops and annual flowers as speedy replacements.
- Replace worn-out plants with divisions of perennials from elsewhere in the garden.
- Sow CCA (cut-and-come-again) salads for a pretty tapestry of colour in just a few weeks.

Planting large borders

Big border, big crop, big impact

Large borders bring both opportunities and dangers. A big space provides the prospect of creating an imposing spectacle, using well-sized plants or generous groups. A substantial crop is also in the offing.

But consider the implications. There may be little need to worry that a plum tree will grow too large, but it can be difficult to get up into the tree to pick the plums. A broad sweep of curly kale looks wonderful in winter, but how much kale do you actually eat?

Choosing plants with impact involves not only thinking about how you will deal with the resulting crops but also how they will look when seen *en masse*. So although the dissected foliage of carrots is attractive close to, from a distance it seems little more than a block of green; this may work in the context of the whole planting, but it may not. Currants, too, look little more than green blobs from a distance, even when in fruit. Fortunately, adding intriguing tints can work surprisingly well from a distance: try the blue-green of leeks or Savoy cabbages or the red of beetroot.

Crops and varieties that remain at their maturity for a long time are important in avoiding a glut when planting in large numbers. For this, leeks are excellent, as are Brussels sprouts, winter cabbage and chards. You can even cheat with red oak-leaf lettuce. It has colourful, prettily lobed leaves and usually develops a relatively flat profile, which is less obvious from a distance than in close-up. Eventually, however, oak-leaf lettuce will start to run to seed and develop a dramatic vertical profile, creating towers of red, purple or bronze up to 60cm (2ft) high. These really show up from across a broad lawn. You need bold ornamentals to go with them. Single plants of perennials or a little group of three violas will make little impact from a distance, but a carpet of red petunias under the purple sprouts will stand out, and with golden hops behind, climbing through a green hedge, and a fat clump of big kniphofias will certainly make a considerable impact.

Graham's top tall crops for big borders

- Columnar apples
- Fennel
- Jerusalem artichokes
- Purple Brussels sprouts
- Rhubarb

Good from a distance and good in close-up

In addition to appearing powerful from a distance and producing plenty of food, large borders have another responsibility. They must also look interesting when seen close-to. There are two ways to achieve this.

The first is by choosing food plants and ornamentals that themselves have close-up appeal as well as long-distance impact. Globe artichokes are a good choice because their jaggedly divided, silvered

Clematis that appreciate hard pruning each spring, like this 'Perle d'Azur', are the most manageable types to train into apple trees as they never get out of hand.

The contrasting shape and colour of these young leeks and 'Lollo Rosso' lettuce make an attractive summer combination; as the lettuce is cut the leeks will expand to fill the space.

leaves are garden-worthy in their own right, in addition to the bold white structure of the plant, which grabs attention from afar. If you need plants with broad leaves, instead of a courgette chose red cabbage or Savoy cabbage, whose leaves themselves are attractive from an early stage. A Rugosa rose yields bright red vitamin C-rich hips in autumn along with interestingly textured and coloured foliage and summer flowers.

The other approach to enhancing short-distance views in larger borders is to make use of some of the techniques that are suitable for small spaces. Clusters of baby leeks may not show up at all from a distance, but just two or three clusters set among red lettuces at the edge of the group make an attractive small-scale association which will not detract from the big picture. Another version of the same approach is to plant climbers near your apple trees. The Tangutica clematis 'Bill MacKenzie' scrambles quickly up into a mature apple tree, and in summer and autumn its profusion of yellow flowers provokes a 'what is that?' response. Then, from much closer, the pretty structure

of the flowers is evident, together with the long-lasting, silvery-whiskered seedheads.

On a more modest level, canary creeper is invaluable. This small-scale version of nasturtium has dainty, prettily lobed leaves and frilly little yellow flowers. When scrambling through purple sprouts, clinging by its twining leaf stalks, canary creeper adds sparkle in close-up yet from a distance does not detract from the bold sprout leaf shape and rich colouring.

Planting raspberries to grow up tall stakes is another approach. They make a bold vertical statement from afar; from nearer the spring flowers and summer fruits are revealed.

Graham's top plants for both distance and close-up

- Artichokes (globe and Jerusalem)
- Raspberries
- Red cabbage
- Rhubarb
- Rugosa roses

Large border

This large scale border is intended to be viewed across a lawn or other open space but to still look good close up. It is backed by a mix of ornamental and productive wall plants including apples, ceanothus and clematis. In front, stately delphiniums and a sprawling hardy geranium blend with both globe and Jerusalem artichokes together with rich purple Brussels sprouts and feathery purple fennel. Frontal plants include lettuce and chards in bold colours and leeks with their striking habit. All are bounded at the edge with an informal hedge of curly green parsley. Plants are chosen both for their impact from a distance as well as their attractive detail.

1 Apple 'Queen Cox'
2 Ceanothus 'Gloire de Versailles'
3 Clematis 'Bill McKenzie'
4 Apple 'Greensleeves'
5 *Rosa rugosa*
6 Delphinium 'Pacific Giants'
7 Jerusalem artichoke
8 Purple sprouts
9 Globe artichokes
10 Purple fennel
11 Geranium 'Orion'
12 Red cos lettuce 'Nymans'
13 Silver chard 'Lucullus'
14 Leeks 'Apollo'
15 Ruby chard 'Rhubarb Chard'
16 Parsley 'Afro'

approx. 12m (40ft)

N

Seasons and successions

In a small garden everyone sees everything – all at once. Every centimetre of ground must be planted to provide colour and crops for as much of the growing season as possible. In a larger space, however, there are more options.

The old country estates often created borders for a single season or for one type of plant – a midsummer border or a peony border. This idea can be developed as self-contained, seasonal all-in-one gardens or plantings, either in the informal mixed-border style or in more formal plantings. All the plants are chosen to be most colourful at a particular season, although many will also appeal at other times of year. These plantings can be like seasonally themed mixed borders, with fruit trees, shrubs, climbers and perennials as well as annual and perennial vegetables and herbs and cane fruits all targeted at a particular season, although drifts of bulbs or hardy annuals can also provide colour during off-seasons.

However, where there is space, more formal all-in-one seasonal gardens are ideal. These are like potagers with the flowers. A potager is a formal garden, like a small-scale version of the garden at Versailles, designed with a year-round structure of paths and evergreens or low ornamental fencing, which have an attractive shape and solidity even when the beds are bare. Potagers are intended for vegetables, and using ornamental varieties improves their appearance enormously.

If you adopt the all-in-one approach and add flowers, you have what you might call a 'flotager': a formal garden, divided into a series of small beds by paths edged with hedges or low fences, and planted with ornamental food plants and with flowers.

The individual plantings can be formal in style, with plants set out in neat rows or less rigid with a more natural intermingling of vegetation. Either way, in off-season the structural elements and the addition of non-food plants make the whole area more colourful and interesting, while at its peak any seasonal flotager will prove an impressive blend of structure, colour and cropping.

Graham's top tips for successional planting

- Follow short-term crops like lettuce with more of the same but perhaps in a different variety.
- Follow overwintered broad beans with lettuce, red cabbage or summer annuals.
- Create an interplanted succession by setting lettuce between sweetcorn; the sweetcorn will fill over and crop when the lettuce is long gone.
- Fading summer crops can be replaced by chrysamthemums or asters bought in flower for the autumn.

These raised beds, edged with vertical boards, and with gravel paths between them, are planted with single-season crops and annuals which can be changed the following year.

Brick paths and edging create a permanent structure, with box hedging and step-over apples providing additional structure in winter.

Shady borders

Good and bad shade

In general, shade is not ideal for food plants but in some cases this is less of a problem than it sounds as there is more than one kind of shade.

Shade from overhanging trees is quite different from shade cast by a wall at the back of a border, because overhanging tree branches cast shade all day; in addition, the canopy tends to prevent rain from penetrating, and the roots of the tree may suck out any moisture which does soak in. This creates

an inhospitable environment, but only if your overhanging tree is an evergreen should you look to plant elsewhere. Spreading evergreen trees, like cedars and evergreen oaks, are a particular problem as conditions here are both dark and dry. In these cases, you could consider siting a shed rather than plants.

In many cases it will prove possible to remove lower branches of large deciduous trees, letting in more light from the side, and to thin branches, allowing dappled light in from above. This is generally a job for a professional tree surgeon. The soil is also sometimes poor under trees, and this can be remedied by building raised beds, perhaps using logs, and bringing in some good soil. Adding organic matter to the soil and installing a trickle irrigation system using a seep hose will also help enormously (*see* page 163). Another trick is to plant low, shade-tolerant groundcover such as pachysandra under trees and to use it to mask planting boxes set among it and planted with impatiens and herbs.

With shade cast by walls and fences, plants are shaded from only one side, so rain can reach the soil easily. As these areas will receive more light than under a tree, a wider range of plants can be grown. In the shade of walls and fences, where the light is good but there is no direct sun, the scope is wide and you need eschew only plants that insist on bright sunshine.

In some gardens shade can be a positive influence, helping prevent leaf crops from running to seed too quickly. Cool conditions often promote leaf growth.

RIGHT: *The shade of a north-facing wall is a more hospitable place for food plants as these apples, chives and golden feverfew demonstrate.*

LEFT: *Shade from nearby trees does not prevent attractive food plants being grown but varieties must be chosen with care.*

Choosing crops and flowers

In shade cast by trees it is vital that there is a good source of moisture; dry shade is a killer. Once that issue has been addressed there is a huge range of ornamental plants that are suitable for such a situation – see moist shade as an opportunity rather than a problem. With food plants, which are more particular, there are two approaches to shade under trees.

First, choose crops that are happy in shade. Top of the list are the fruits derived from wild plants that grow naturally in shade or the edge of woods and copses – principally strawberries and raspberries but also blueberries, currants and gooseberries. Rhubarb is also a good option. Among vegetables lettuce, pak choi, spinach, beetroot, calabrese, kale and kohl rabi are worth trying and also, among the herbs, parsley, chives and mint. Rampant mint is usually more restrained in shade.

Second, consider that for half the year deciduous trees will carry no leaves and a great deal of light will penetrate. Therefore, crops that develop during winter will be well established and in their final phases of seasonal growth by the time the leaf canopy closes in on them. Thus, broad beans, spring cabbage and winter lettuce are good choices under deciduous trees.

Unsuitable for shade are crops that insist on sun – both for good growth and to develop their flavour. They include tomatoes and sweet peppers, passion fruits, onions, seakale and a number of herbs, such as rosemary and basil.

There is an extensive range of ornamentals to go with crops in improved shade under trees. This is just a tantalizing selection: honeysuckles, camellias, rhododendrons, pieris, maples, hostas, hardy geraniums, foxgloves, primroses, hellebores, pulmonarias, wood anemones, snowdrops, violets, honesty, toad lilies, ferns and impatiens.

In the shade of walls, where there is no direct sun, a vast range of ornamentals will thrive. Among those from which you can choose are: daffodils and other spring bulbs, forsythia, foxgloves, lamium, ornamental grasses, pulmonarias, violas and weigela.

Graham's top ten shade-tolerant food plants

- Broad beans
- Lettuce
- Mint
- Mizuna greens
- Pak choi
- Parsley
- Raspberries
- Rhubarb
- Spinach
- Strawberries

In a cool, shady corner this wild strawberry is flowering prettily with silvery sedums and will soon develop its small sweet red fruits.

Shady border

A north facing border may seem an unlikely situation for food plants but many will thrive. Here a fence is clothed in silvery ivy, quince and fragrant osmanthus, making a fine background for clumps of upright foxgloves. The main food plants in this mixed border are berried fruits whose wild ancestors tend to grow in partial shade. Currants, gooseberries, raspberries and strawberries feature strongly along with shade loving perennials like hellebores and hostas. This is an especially good site for summer sown CCA crops which appreciate a break from the daylong sun.

1 Ivy (*Hedera helix* 'Glacier')
2 Quince
3 *Osmanthus delavayi*
4 Raspberry (red berries)
5 Raspberry (yellow berries)
6 Blackcurrant
7 Redcurrant
8 Gooseberry
9 Strawberry

10 Alpine strawberry
11 *Helleborus* X *hybridus*
12 Hosta 'June'
13 CCA mixture
14 *Sarcococca confusa*
15 Curly parsley
16 Lettuce 'Red Salad Bowl'
17 Foxgloves 'Camelot Mixed'

approx. 6m (20ft)

Dry and sunny borders

Less dry, more options

Drought is likely to be something that everyone has to think about, and fortunately all-in-one gardeners are in a good position to deal with the situation. Unless they are unusually stony or rocky, dry, it is not difficult to turn sunny borders into areas that are a great deal less dry – and thus far more hospitable to plants. Most often, especially if the dry garden is on a slope, the change is an improvement rather than a transformation. Organic matter and moisture are the key factors in making this change.

Digging in garden compost, used potting compost, soil improvers from the garden centre or well-rotted manure assists in the retention of moisture and provides plant foods over a long period. It also helps build the depth of soil – many borders are dry not only because they are exposed to the sun but also because the soil is shallow and poor.

Slopes are notoriously dry as the water simply drains away. By making terraces (as is so often done for vineyards and olive groves), an increased depth of soil is provided and moisture run-off prevented. Use the materials that suit your taste and the style of your garden: for example, stones, vertical boards or logs.

Supplying extra moisture by irrigation requires more thought. Ideally, as water becomes a more precious commodity, you should try to use less on the garden. However, watering makes such a dramatic difference to so many crops that food plants should be the last plants from which it is withdrawn. However, using a sprinkler is folly, because such a high proportion of the water simply evaporates into the air. Instead, you should install a seep hose (*see* page 163).

Graham's top tips for turning dry soil into damp

- Add organic matter, such as garden compost or well-rotted manure.
- Run seep hoses for watering (and never use sprinklers).
- Turn slopes into terraces.

Raised beds that are built using pressure-treated boards will last for years and when constructed as terracing, as here, provide an ideal solution to gardening on a slope.

Dry Garden

Sheltered by fences or walls, with an arbour over the seat, Mediterranean and Mediterranean-style plants predominate with a structure of evergreen shrubs, especially ornamental herbs. A fig, olive, nectarine and vine provide fruits, a tapestry of creeping thymes edges an opening across the gravel and is punctuated by sages and helianthemums. The whole area is mulched in gravel with various hardy annuals like California poppies, nigellas and horned poppies (not indicated individually) self sowing where they will. Dwarf bulbs like crocus and iris are scattered through in spring.

1 Vine over the arbour
2 Ceanothus 'Puget Blue'
3 *Passiflora caerulea*
4 *Coronilla valentina* 'Citrina'
5 Fig
6 Sweet pea 'Cupani'
7 Nectarine
8 *Ipomoea* 'Heavenly Blue'
9 *Phlomis italica*
10 Rosemary 'Miss Jessops Upright'
11 Rosemary Prostratus Group
12 Sage 'Purpurascens'
13 Helianthemum 'Rhodanthe Carneum', Wisley White' and various pastel shades.
14 Euphorbia 'Lambrook Gold'
15 Euphorbia 'Portuguese Velvet'
16 *Cistus* X *cyprius*
17 Lavender 'Little Lottie'
18 Lavender 'Hidcote Giant'
19 Zauschneria 'Western Hills'
20 Thyme (creeping, various)
21 Olive in tub
22 Lemon in tub
23 Sage 'Berggarten'

approx. 12m (40ft)

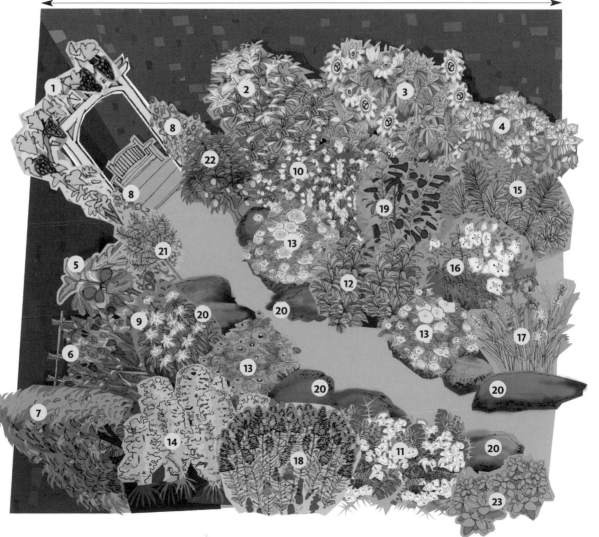

N

Choose natural drought-lovers

If a situation is naturally hot and dry, usually because a gravelly, well-drained soil has been exposed to sun, you should always seek to work with such conditions by choosing appropriate plants, even if you also decide to try to and improve the soil. Correct plant choice is crucial.

In such hot, dry positions grapes naturally come to mind. You can choose between genuine outdoor fruiting types and those whose fruit is less scrumptious but that have more ornamental appeal. Around the vines sow seeds of annual climbers like old-fashioned Grandiflora sweet peas, which originate in the Mediterranean climate of Sicily. They will climb through the grapevine to provide a winning combination. Figs too will relish the conditions.

Think about other plants you see in the Mediterranean. One of the reasons Mediterranean tomatoes taste so good is the combination of sun and dryish soil found in that region. Yet without rich feeding and constant moisture, yields can be low; it is often a trade-off. Seakale, which grows naturally on shingle beaches – not much soil or shade there – is another winner. It looks lovely with big bushy euphorbias, along with globe artichokes and cardoons, onions and garlic. Yet in all these cases, intensity of flavour may be at the expense of a high yield. Crops with naturally deep-questing roots like melons and pumpkins should also thrive (although they do appreciate a good soak), and are wonderful cascading down terraces. As partners, sun-loving shrubs, like cistus, phlomis, coronilla and euphorbias, can provide evergreen structure. Achilleas, sedums, rock roses and brooms give a long season of interest, and annuals like California poppies, linarias, baby zinnias and horned poppies will self-sow, creating unexpected associations, year after year.

A more structured approach to hot, dry borders is also possible. In gravel, plant thymes as edging around a closed canopy of rosemaries, lavenders and santolinas plus cistus and rock roses, all organized in a more formal fashion.

Graham's top five drought-tolerant crops
- Figs
- Grapes
- Rosemary
- Seakale
- Thymes

Herbs love the sun

The most obvious plants for a sunny, dry situation are herbs, especially Mediterranean ones. All-in-one gardeners can create a whole Mediterranean planting with the focus on ornamental herbs. These work beautifully as a visual picture regardless of their practical use. Rosemary, sage, lavender and thyme alone probably have hundreds of ornamental variants

RIGHT: *Figs are ideal on a warm sunny wall and can either be trained formally or allowed to develop into a more informal shape.*

FAR RIGHT: *The broad foliage of a row of developing plants of crisp lettuce and the fine grey lavender foliage are enlivened bold and bright French marigolds.*

The soft purple leaves of this ornamental sage are ideal partnered with the glossy leaves and red, rounded flowerheads of Sedum telephium 'Atropurpureum' *in a sunny border.*

with coloured leaves, a range of growth habits and flowers in different colours. All are evergreen, providing genuine year-round interest. Rosemary in particular will often flower in mild spells in winter.

It is fun to bring these herbs together with the shrubs with which they grow naturally – such as cistus, rock roses, phlomis, coronilla and euphorbias, even an olive, perhaps in a pot – as well as with plants from the Americas that enjoy a similar habitat like the California fuchsia (*Zauschneria*), ceanothus and climbing mutisias. The excitement mounts when annuals and biennials are added to the mix.

There are, though, practical aspects to consider, in particular access within the border. These plants all look good when mulched with gravel or chippings (nothing too white); this shows them off well and helps prevent the more susceptible from succumbing to rots in unusually wet winters. Access is important: you need to be able to get in among the plants to nip off shoots for the kitchen without this being too much of a struggle.

If a slope has been terraced, you might decide to place narrow gravel paths at the foot of each retaining wall. Otherwise, flat pieces of natural stone that tone with the mulch can be laid to provide paths or vantage points. Set them either in an informal pattern, alongside herbs to which you need access or in a slightly camouflaged, curved path, with spaces between the stones. Lay the stones just a fraction below gravel level so they blend in well.

A sunny herb garden can also be laid out formally, like a Mediterranean potager, in which case paving slabs are more appropriate and will produce a look that is more modern in style.

Graham's top ten partners for Mediterranean herbs

- Ceanothus
- Cistus
- Coronilla
- Crocus (species)
- Euphorbia
- Fig
- Grapevine
- Helianthemum
- Olive
- Zauschneria

Raised beds

Productivity plus

Growing food in raised beds is the most productive and also one of the most attractive forms of vegetable, herb and fruit cultivation. Based on traditional systems used, for example, in the west of Ireland for hundreds of years, crops are grown in rectangular beds no more than 1.2m (4ft) wide so they can be tended comfortably from each side. Raised beds also allow the intensive underplanting of edible plants with flowers.

The beds are raised by the generous addition of organic matter. In the all-in-one setting the beds look most elegant if they are edged, for example with vertical boards, which can be stained, or with bricks or stone. The path areas alongside and between the beds can also be given a decorative and durable surface.

Crops should be grown in short rows across the beds. This is attractive, discourages gluts by making you think about each short row you sow, allows different crops and flowers to be grown alongside each other in a wide range of combinations, and gives you access to every plant without getting your feet muddy. Even traditional varieties look good when grown by this unusually productive method.

The all-in-one version based on ornamental vegetable and herb varieties can be augmented by fruit – in patches, in rows or as individual specimens – and by flowers. Cut flowers and plants cultivated for their cut foliage look wonderful when grown in rows across neatly edged rectangular beds between tidy rows of attractive vegetables.

With this intensive method, plants are grown more closely than usual. If more than one row of a particular variety is cultivated, the plants can be staggered at equal spacing, as this has been shown to provide the best crop from a given area. Thorough soil preparation, therefore, is essential.

Deeply worked organic matter is the key factor in producing prolific, good-looking crops from a small space without too much watering and too many applications of fertilizer. Prepare the beds as thoroughly as you can manage by working garden compost, well-rotted manure, used potting compost or soil improvers evenly through the whole depth of the bed. Never leave soil conditioners in a lump at the bottom of the trench (*see* page 160).

RIGHT: *Pale teal blue stained boards make an ideal edging to rows of different vegetables. Here red looseleaf lettuce retains its shape while the tall green lettuce grows up in a bold pillar.*

LEFT: *Raised beds can be built quickly using logroll. Here the beds make a bold and productive garden feature with standard marguerites, ornamental kales and lettuce.*

Style and materials

Raised beds look best when given an interesting edging. The simplest, most adaptable and potentially the most attractive edging is made from pressure-treated timber set on edge. Start by marking out the area with canes and some string, then prepare the bed as described below (*see also* page 161).

Choose 15 x 2.5cm (6 x 1in) boards treated against rot with environmentally safe preservative. Then stain them a colour to suit your taste, the material you have in mind for your path and the style of your garden. The boards can be positioned to make simple rectangular beds up to 1.2m (4ft) wide and up to about 5m (15ft) long. Secure them against vertical 5 x 2.5cm (2 x 1in) posts knocked in on the inside and held in place by two brass or chrome-plated screws from the outside. Boards can also be used to make interesting patterns; and long boards can be bent into gentle curves, the posts holding them in place. For less mobile and less agile gardeners, even those in wheelchairs, rather higher raised beds can be invaluable. When beds are raised to 60cm (2ft), even 90cm (3ft), it is much easier to look after the plants. High raised beds are also the answer in gardens where the soil is unimprovable or where deep concrete cannot practicably be removed.

Other materials that may be suitable for edging a raised bed include rustic logs laid horizontally; narrower logs knocked in vertically; terracotta roofing tiles set on edge; bricks or brick-like concrete blocks; and stone or synthetic stone. It is a matter of taste and

matching, or consciously contrasting, the style of the surroundings. In modern courtyard gardens, rendered blockwork painted white, or another colour, looks crisp and clean and shows off dark foliage well.

Finishing touches

The more carefully you prepare a raised bed, the better the crops and the less maintenance they will need. Once the boards have been stained and set in place around the prepared soil, or the stones or bricks laid dry, the soil should be raked and worked to give a flat final finish. In most areas watering will be necessary at some point during the season, so at this stage perforated seep hoses can be laid 15cm (6in) apart on the soil surface but under the mulch if there is one.

Graham's top tips for raised beds
- Add plenty of well-rotted organic material to retain moisture.
- Choose an interesting material with which to edge the beds.
- Grow plants in short rows or in patches.

Raised bed

This raised bed is made by setting long, 15cm (6in) wide stained boards on edge to create a 1.2m (4ft) wide bed. Sited in an open place, tall cactus-flowered dahlias provide cut flowers at the south end and also shade for nearby leaf crops. Other annual cut flowers such as nigella, salvias and cornflowers are set alongside colourful vegetables including bush tomatoes, cabbage, lettuce while the CCA salad crop benefits from a little shade from dwarf runner beans. Crops for winter can be planted as these summer crops fade, or the whole bed cleared at the end of the season and prepared for spring sown crops the following year.

1 Parsley 'Afro'
2 Chives
3 CCA mixed salads blend
4 Runner bean 'Hestia'
5 Cornflower 'Florence Blue'
6 Red beet 'MacGregor's Favourite'
7 Bush tomato 'Tornado'

8 *Salvia farinacea* 'Victoria'
9 Red cabbage 'Redsky'
10 Nigella 'Miss Jekyll'
11 Red lettuce 'Sioux'
12 Coriander (cilantro)
13 Dahlia 'Cactus Hybrids'

approx. 1.2m (4ft)

Integration

You can grow a huge range of plants in a raised bed. It is simplest, and some would say the most attractive over time, to plant side-by-side rows and small blocks of relatively short-term ornamental vegetable and herb varieties as well as cut flowers. Seed of coloured-leaf lettuces, clarkia, dwarf beans (chosen also for their good flowers), curly parsley and more can be sown in rows across the bed, the plants thinned, allowed to mature and then picked or cut. Fun can be had with

patterns too. Dark-leaved beets or chards can be set in a zigzag row along the bed and compact flowers, like bedding geraniums, planted in the triangles.

Tall plants like climbing beans, which produce such a large crop that the discipline of thinking about every row you plant is an invaluable restraint, can provide summer shade for plants like coriander (cilantro) and spinach, which tend to run to seed if exposed to hot sun. Or perhaps you could plant a row of three tall, shade-producing dahlias for cutting.

Purple Brussels sprouts, just two or three plants across the bed, look superb with late-summer crocosmias for cutting, while variegated dwarf box in a row across the bed creates an air of permanence and structure and provides shelter on a windy site.

Strawberries need a more permanent place, although to keep them cropping well they are best replaced after three years; plant them in a block of staggered rows. A row of raspberries across the bed is a long-term, permanent planting. Two or three different varieties can be used as dividers along the bed, or one variety placed at just one end, perhaps where there is a little shade from a neighbour's tree.

Tree fruit can also go in a raised bed, but there is always the risk that a tree's shade and its thirsty roots will have a detrimental effect on too extensive a stretch of a neighbouring bed. Tree fruit is better used as a focal point in the garden as a whole. It can be trained flat as a cordon on a fence or wires to give backing to a bed. Low step-over apples can be used as edging.

RIGHT: *Timber edging supports extra depth of soil and looks good planted with black Tuscan and curly kale plus purple Brussels sprouts, all backed by contrasting fine-leaved white cosmos.*

LEFT: *These red and green lettuces – some mature, some developing well and some relatively recently planted – will between them crop over a long period. The nasturtiums are being guided into them to create an attractive picture.*

Container planting

Containers and uses

Some of the most impressive, and productive, all-in-one planting schemes can be created in containers. When used in very small spaces especially, containers tend to be the focus of attention. You can water and feed well, dead-head and harvest almost daily, and pests and diseases can be spotted and dealt with before they take hold. Combine this with high-quality potting compost and good drainage, which is so easy to provide, and the result is a display that both looks attractive and is tasty. When planted with seasonal crops and set amid the all-in-one garden, pots add an extra dimension, yet they are readily removed and replaced when their interest subsides. Containers are most definitely a moveable feast.

The range of possibilities is certainly wide, from a single, purple basil plant in a clay pot among pots of bedding geraniums, to a 60cm (2ft) wide tub, which needs more than a whole bag of potting compost and will nurture a fruit tree to maturity.

Tubs, half-barrels, urns and large planting boxes

For focal points on the patio or deck, on either side of the front door, alongside seats, on balconies and roof gardens, large containers provide both root space and impact for a wide range of plantings based on, for example, tall tomatoes, climbing beans, aubergines, fruit trees and vines with morning glories, hardy or ivy-leaved bedding geraniums , hostas, cannas, fennel and roses. Another advantage is that tubs of flowers can be moved anywhere in the garden as a quick and easy way to add colour and interest and fill gaps created by partial harvesting or by the end of a seasonal crop.

Graham's container recipes for tall combinations in large containers
- Citrus with scented-leaved bedding geraniums.
- Climbing bean 'Painted Lady' with 'Heavenly Blue' morning glory.
- 'Queen Cox' apple with hardy geraniums or alpine strawberries.
- Tall tomatoes with canary creeper.

Troughs

These are useful for edging the patio or deck. Build your own from pressure-treated timber if possible and make them deeper and wider than most shop-bought troughs. Stain them the colour of choice or leave them to 'silver' naturally with age. Troughs are good for small cut-and-come-again salad crops and small herbs such as thyme or parsley combined with neat-flowered plants like begonias and impatiens.

Window-boxes

Build these as for troughs, and then place them on sills outside windows that open vertically or on brackets on fences. Plant with drought- and wind-tolerant plants like sage, alyssum and edible nasturtiums.

Variegated sage, yellow French marigolds and trailing bush tomatoes make this hanging basket both colourful and productive.

Graham's container recipes for troughs and window-boxes

- Curly parsley with dwarf, lemon yellow French marigolds or (in shade) white impatiens.
- Cut-and-come-again salads in colourful blends.
- Round-rooted carrots with violas.
- Variegated thymes and wild crocus (especially for window-boxes).

Hanging baskets

Hanging baskets are excellent anywhere above head height and out of the wind, especially by doors and windows. Set up a drip watering system, if possible, to help keep them consistently moist. Some tomato varieties have been bred specially for baskets, and these can be blended with many trailing summer flowers, such as lobelia and bacopa. Small-growing strawberry varieties are also suitable for hanging baskets. Whether plastic, or preferably wire, baskets add a whole new style and elegance to the all-in-one garden, adding colour and interest in new situations. Plant through the sides as well as from the top and feed the plants well.

Graham's container recipes for hanging baskets

- Curly parsley with white or pale pink mini petunias.
- Trailing rosemary with lobelia.
- Trailing tomatoes with white bacopa or yellow lysimachia.

Growing bags

These compost-filled plastic bags can nurture tomatoes, peppers and other crops. Low, spreading annuals like impatiens can be used to hide the plastic.

Steel planters

Galvanized planters – even bins – are good in hot situations, especially if polished, as they reflect heat and so keep roots cool. Use red cabbage and trailing scarlet petunias to contrast with their silver finish.

Concrete planters

These are relatively inexpensive and come in a wide range of shapes and sizes to suit most design styles, although shallow planters dry out quickly.

Terracotta pots

Individual terracotta pots, 13–20cm (5–8in) wide, are suitable for single herb plants or small vegetables. Intermingle them with pots of bedding geraniums or baby petunias or, in shade, hostas, hardy geraniums and impatiens. They will need watering daily.

Plastic pots

Although these need less watering than terracotta pots most plastic pots look less elegant. Fortunately, once plants mature, the pots should be hidden.

Strawberry pots

These tall terracotta pots have openings in the side for planting. Parsley and white mini petunias look great together in them, as do herbs (or, or course, strawberries). Strawberry pots need a great deal of water.

Graham's top five good container specimens
- Blueberries
- Bushy crab apples
- Citrus
- Figs
- Peaches, apricots and nectarines

RIGHT: *Citrus trees are ideal in containers and can be left outside in mild areas or moved into shelter in colder gardens. A foamy Erigeron karvinskianus fills the pot at the base.*

LEFT: *The marrow's bold foliage and bright fruit make a great feature in this large, polished, galvanised pot although you will need to water regularly.*

Fruit trees as productive specimens

Large tubs and half-barrels are ideal for tree fruit. Planting a fruit tree in a tub often allows you to grow fruit where it would not otherwise be possible – in a small garden, perhaps, or on the patio – and the very fact that the roots are restricted keeps the tree to a manageable size.

For most apples, pears, plums, cherries, crab apples and figs a 60cm (2ft) wide container filled with fresh, sterile, soil-based potting compost is ideal. Never use garden soil. Some cherries and crab apples are naturally dwarf and can be planted in a smaller container if necessary, as can citrus bushes, dwarf peaches and nectarines. A vine will also thrive in a pot if it has somewhere to climb and can be supported. Autumn raspberries are excellent, and need support, too. Blueberries are perhaps the perfect container fruits as they need lime-free soil, which can be bought in a bag (most garden soil is limey), and provide three seasons of colour.

The trick when planting tubs and half-barrels is to choose planting partners for the fruit tree or bush that complement it but that do not smother it or steal too much moisture and nutrients.

Options for the edge of the container depend on how much sun it receives and how assiduous you are with watering and feeding. Try, for example, curly parsley, white trailing lobelia, strawberries, hanging basket tomatoes, thyme, impatiens, small hardy geraniums, trailing rosemary or petunias. Annual climbers, such as morning glory, convolvulus and mina (*Ipomoea lobata*) can be invaluable, too.

One of the great advantages of growing fruits in containers is that their restricted roots keep the trees and bushes small, making it easier to cover them and therefore protect the fruit from birds. Use fine, black netting, which is relatively invisible.

Graham's top five fruits for pots

- Blueberries
- Citrus
- Dwarf peaches
- Figs
- Olives

On the balcony

Balconies provide particular advantages but also pose special problems. Intense sunshine and heat can be an advantage, as can the fact that you tend to be in close contact with the plants every day. However, that same heat can be too fierce and the wind too strong for many plants to thrive.

Some plants do revel in the sun and heat: vines, peaches, nectarines, tomatoes, peppers, olives, bananas and Mediterranean herbs, like sage, rosemary and basil. Combine them with petunias, calibrachoas, California poppies, morning glory, bedding geraniums, osteospermums and cannas plus hardy succulents like aeoniums. The sun and heat must be balanced by constant moisture. If water is

LEFT: *On this high roof-terrace a dwarf pine provides year-round interest. Verbena is added for summer colour and scarlet peppers provide both colour and a little hot flavour.*

needed every day, then regular feeding is also crucial as frequent watering washes nutrients away.

A better situation for a wider range of plants is a balcony that receives sun for only part of the day, ideally in the evening. This allows the walls to heat up and retain heat which is released at night but avoids the plants being scorched all day.

Balconies are often subject to strong winds, and broad-leaved plants like bananas and those with relatively fragile leaves like tomatoes can be damaged or dry out in spite of having moist roots. Wind helps pollinate tomatoes yet tends to deter bees, so fruit trees on windy balconies may need help to set fruit. A cheap artist's paint brush ruffled in flower after flower will do

RIGHT: *Black planters with purple-leaved fennel and white roses make a dramatic patio combination for a modern setting.*

the job; peaches and nectarines need this in many situations. If you want just one tree, choose a variety that does not require a different variety as pollinator.

Being in close contact with your plants, just outside the living room or bedroom, perhaps, will ensure you check them over regularly and of course you'll only need to carry the watering can a few steps to and from the balcony (check that it does not drip on to hardwood floors or carpets).

Graham's top tips for balconies
- Choose heat-loving plants that withstand the wind.
- Feed frequently.
- Water daily.

Patios and entrances

Patios and entrances are natural sites for tubs and baskets. Both positions allow you to bring container-grown plants into a new situation and maximize space. In such prominent positions, however, it is crucial that the containers look good all season; drab plantings and ragged presentations are unacceptable, so make sure you tidy them regularly.

The containers must be large enough to take the potting compost required to grow your chosen plants and to retain plenty of moisture and nutrients. Tubs must be of good quality and not cracked. They should be clean or acceptably aged or algaed, with good drainage holes, and raised off the ground on attractive or invisible feet to maximize drainage.

On patios and in entrances, hanging baskets should be deep and hung on stout chains fixed securely in a position where they will not be knocked or impede passers-by. Pack wire baskets with a foam or hessian liner, or possibly fresh moss, and select plastic baskets for their style, capacity and solidity – not for their price. Choose a long-season potting compost specifically formulated for containers and add a slow-release fertilizer. As feeding is crucial, it should preferably be at least partially automated to ensure it really does happen.

Cherry tomatoes make good feature plants and are easy to grow. Just one tall type looks good in the centre of a large tub, for example, or plant three dwarf trailing types round the edge with a yellow argyranthemum in the centre. Cherry tomatoes are also suitable for a hanging basket. Their little yellow-green flowers are intriguing in close-up and the strings of fruits provide colour and food over a very long season. Add annual climbers to tall tomato types; use purple basil in hot situations, or medium-height, single French marigolds to cover the bare bases of tomato stems. In hanging baskets add blue and white lobelia, white bacopa or yellow lysimachia.

An impressive alternative is to to keep the planting scheme simple by setting a single specimen fruit tree in a large tub. A bushy crab apple works very well as a centrepiece, as does a lemon tree. In a more

prominent situation a simple, shallow-rooted, evergreen groundcover, like pink-flowered dead nettle, is ideal underneath, its prettily white-striped leaves boosted by pink flowers while the tree is carrying its white blossom. A bay tree makes a superb container plant and can be decorated with fairy-lights. The leaves release a lovely aroma when they are crushed.

Watering and feeding

Watering and feeding are the two most crucial elements of the care of any plants in containers. And with food crops in particular the need to get it right cannot be overestimated.

Of course, you can carry cans of water down the path every day. This is less of a struggle if you install an outside tap so that cans need not be carried through the house. But once you have a water supply outside, there is an alternative watering method, which does not involve carrying cans and is relatively easy to set up. A ring of seep hoses or drip nozzles on unobtrusive, narrow-gauge, black-plastic pipework, which can be clipped in place along a fence or wall, can be attached to the mains water. You will need just one drip nozzle in a hanging basket and three to five nozzles in a 60cm (2ft) pot or large tub. The tap can be operated manually, or an automatic timer can be set to open the flow regularly and so ensure that the roots stay moist. Automatic liquid feeders can be installed in the water pipeline, but they are comparatively expensive.

Galvanised steel containers planted with tomatoes and nasturtiums combine to look very stylish in a contemporary garden.

Mulching is as invaluable in retaining moisture in containers as it is in the garden. Bark mulches can be used, but birds tend to fling bark all over the paving so gravel is generally a better choice and will also help deter slugs. If you choose gravel in larger sizes, about 2cm (³/₄in) across, for example, weed seeds will rarely establish themselves in the containers.

Your first opportunity for feeding is before planting, when you can add a slow-release granular fertilizer to the compost. Then each spring work slow-release fertilizer pellets into the top few centimetres of compost. Adding slow-release granular fertilizer to the compost works well for a few weeks or months, but a weekly liquid feeding from a watering can will eventually become necessary through the growing season. For this, a liquid tomato food is ideal. The brand is immaterial but a tomato food that is designed to encourage a heavy and tasty crop of tomatoes will work the same way for other fruits and for flowers as well. Long-term plants, such as fruit trees, will require feeding throughout their lives.

Graham's top tips for containers

- Employ drip nozzles whenever possible.
- Install an outside water tap.
- Keep plants well fed.
- Mulch with gravel.
- Use water-retentive container compost.

03 | Seasonal Food and Flowers

Creating a garden that is impressive all year round is the aim of almost every gardener. Bringing flowers and food plants together in the all-in-one garden not only increases the opportunities but also, of course, adds the element of the year-round harvest.

Spring, summer, autumn, winter and back to spring again bring a cascade of colour and produce, attractive plants and eye-catching planting combinations, striking structures and seasonal effects with plenty of flavoursome food and aromatic herbs in a constantly interesting garden.

Of course, there is a challenge in making this happen. Inevitably there is more to it than simply planting tomatoes in gaps in the flower border and hoping for the best, but the following season-by-season discussion will provide some invaluable ideas.

In late summer, bright ornamental kale and feathery dill are partnered by rich pink lavateras and a neat edging of pink petunias in a thoughtful, colour co-ordinated display.

Spring in the all-in-one garden

Spring is an exciting time for the all-in-one gardener. As the months go by, more crops become ready for picking, and more are sown and planted to provide a harvest later in the year. Fruit blossom is at its peak, and at the same time the range of flowers and foliage plants increases daily and is at its best alongside the fruit trees. The result is a profusion of food, flowers and combinations of the two.

Structure

The pattern of a garden's structure, perhaps created by box hedges, softens as pale new shoots light up the dark lines, while on walls and fences and on wires fruit blossom marks out the comforting regular patterns of the branches.

The lines of paving, too, start to soften soften as oregano spills over and creeping thyme expands along the joints in the bricks. Seedlings of many annuals, like opium poppies and California poppies, make pretty colours and shapes against bricks or gravel, but some may need removing as they grow larger. Along straight paths bordering the potager, step-over apple trees are in bloom, creating an attractive floral border.

Walls and fences

Flurries of carmine-backed, white apple blossoms and white pear blossoms open earliest on walls, then on fences and finally on wires. Those sweet peas at the base are growing strongly and may need a little guidance to encourage their tendrils to cling. In front, the elegant arching curves of the pink-and-white bleeding hearts (*Dicentra spectabilis*) tone in beautifully with the apple flowers, and their lush stems with the self-sown forget-me-nots and rosettes of coriander, as well as the strawberries at the base, benefit from the protection from frost that the wall provides.

Figs are breaking away from their bold winter outline with fresh leaves, and the overwintered fruits start to swell, so they must not go short of water.

Fruit trees

Crab apples too are at peak blossom, which continues for longer than culinary apples. If you choose to plant an eating or cooking apple variety that is not self-fertile (*see* pages 102–103), like the excellent 'James Grieve', the crab apple will pollinate it and other apple varieties flowering later in spring. A blue-flowered spring clematis trained up into the crab apple will provide extra colour in the same garden site, while a mature tree, its bark clothed with a yellow-leaved hop, makes a striking image.

Citrus moved into a porch or conservatory for winter protection will start to grow as the days lengthen; feeding, watering and a check for pests will then be necessary. Such plants can be moved outside to a sheltered place in late spring, but do try to accustom them gradually to outdoor life. The new growth on grapevines will need guidance and perhaps tying in, as it develops strongly in spring.

Crab apples are ideal trees for the all-in-one garden, their spring flowers are followed by fruits in autumn and they can be grown in the garden or in containers.

Beds and borders

By spring the leeks have gone and the kale is erupting with new growth as the daffodils flower around it. The kale may also soon see its last days as raggedness begins to dominate beauty. In the all-in-one garden other spring bulbs open in pretty – and sometimes surprising – colour combinations: blue scillas or blue or white muscari with red chicory; white puschkinias with mizuna greens; more daffodils with red or orange chard and yellow-leaved oregano.

At some point from late spring onwards, when the bulbs are dormant and the veg crop is gone, it is a good idea to dig up the bulbs and replant them deeply. They have a tendency to work their way towards the surface over the years and risk being damaged by a trowel when you plant over them.

Autumn-sown broad beans will be flowering and may need support as the pods develop. In front, young red cabbage plants have gone in, and a carpet of green cut-and-come-again (CCA) salads is rapidly maturing underneath. By the time the CCA crop is over, the prolific blue *Geranium* 'Orion' will have stretched among the cabbage from behind.

Now is the time to move a few silvery blue, double opium poppy seedlings among 'Lollo Rossa' lettuce and dainty short white daffodils to take over once the lettuce is cut and the daffodils fade. Alongside, rapidly emerging chives look good with golden oregano and chocolate-leaved *Heuchera micrantha* var. *diversifolia* 'Palace Purple' or a newer, prettily patterned variety.

Raised beds

Raised beds start to liven up as spring-planted and spring-sown crops and flowers develop rapidly. Red and green lettuces (looseleaf and hearty), newly planted chards in their sparkling individual colours, beets, red cabbages, onions and spring onions, broad beans and more are interplanted with rows of shorter, hardy annual cut flowers.

These annuals can be raised in plug trays in the same way as many vegetables (*see* page 165). Choose the shorter varieties of clarkia, cornflowers, godetia, lavatera, nigella and dwarf red-flowered amaranthus with its ruby foliage. Many will have been sown and planted in autumn, with the salads and other food crops sown or planted between them in spring. Together they will produce a prolific display rather early in the season, unless the winter is especially ferocious. The combination of flowers and foliage is delightful.

There are other crops, including CCA salads, which can be sown or planted in early spring and will quickly produce edibles. Spring onions can be sown directly into a border. Their red forms are lovely alongside jagged-leaved mizuna greens, which can also be sown in early spring. The fresh green feathery foliage of baby round carrots, sown direct or, preferably, planted out in plugs containing clusters of seedlings, is ideal alongside beets or around a dark-leaved, neatly lobed heuchera. Heuchera leaves can be picked for posies.

Onion sets should be planted now, as should leeks sown in plug trays. Lettuce planted in plugs alongside either vegetable creates a contrast of upright, rounded onion leaves and low, colourful rosettes.

The vegetable tapestry

Because they are ready in just a few weeks, CCA salad mixes or individual varieties can be sown around a range of longer-term crops like chard or cabbages, or around developing, clump-forming perennials like hostas or irises; choose the exact variety or mix to create the best look. CCA salad is also a great crop to sow when you have an empty patch that will be planted with a major crop later in the season, because it quickly starts to look pretty.

Around the patio or deck, give CCA salad a block of its own or fill a trough or window-box and snip over a section of leaves at a time. Alternatively, grow them in two or three troughs, sown at different times, and move them around so the best-looking trough is always the most prominent.

Mediterranean herbs

Among the Mediterranean herbs, rosemary is in full flower in spring and golden thyme is at its most brilliant, while overwintered annuals like California poppies develop prettily cut, often silvered foliage and brilliant, saucer-shaped flowers. They look wonderful peeping through the gold-edged leaves of 'Icterina' sage. Everything has the freshness of spring as bulbs such as wild tulips emerge and flare above flowering carpets of creeping thyme.

Elegant creamy tulips add spring colour to the lettuce in this informal sunny country border; they can be followed by bushy tomatoes.

Self-sown seedlings of flowering annuals and herbs – and also of weeds – begin to appear in the gravel, often a little too prolifically. Learning to distinguish between weeds and more useful plants can be tricky, so watch and learn. Some of the profusion of 'good' seedlings must be pulled out, along with the weeds. Others, however, can be transplanted easily when they are small and moved to places where they will associate well with the more established plants around them. At the same time, self-sown perennials that may become overvigorous for the all-in-one garden should be removed.

Move tiny California poppy seedlings alongside the golden oregano and silvery-leaved horned poppy near the purple sage. But remember, one of the reasons these plants do well in dry conditions is that they send down a deep root, which is easily broken unless you move the seedlings while they are small.

Around the patio and deck

Scent is another dimension to keep in mind when you are selecting plant varieties for the patio and deck. Attention to plant care should ensure that these areas, where plants are constantly seen from unusually close quarters, are always appealing.

Chards will keep their foliage well through the winter if planted in a sheltered position at the front of patio borders, but any damaged leaves must be removed as they surge into growth, with bright tulips among them. In this situation, as they eventually run

Out on the deck this white-flowering crab apple is partnered by trailing ivies with the addition, for spring, of columbines and fragrant hyacinths.

to seed, they can be replaced with more chard or with bush tomatoes and, perhaps, calibrachoas.

The stems of climbers, as well as wall and fence shrubs, need to be organized carefully so that their branches are evenly and elegantly spread out. Early spring is the last chance to do this before they begin to grow strongly. Be sure to protect hostas from slugs before their shoots emerge, as once those new leaves are damaged they will not repair themselves. Sow 'Red Salad Bowl' lettuce as a CCA crop around blue-leaved varieties, to be cropped two or three times before the hosta leaves are fully expanded.

The sheltered conditions of the patio or deck allow tender plants to be put outside a little sooner than would be possible in the open garden. Tomatoes and peppers, plus half-hardy annuals like petunias and impatiens, will appreciate the extra week or two in the ground, although they will need covering with fleece to protect them during frosty weather.

Containers

In containers, blueberries will be flowering in spring, showing off their dainty white bells. Give them regular feeding with fertilizer for acid-loving plants. Other permanent container plants will also enjoy regular feeding; choose either a shrub food or a tomato food. As pot-grown plants are now growing strongly, watering becomes crucial.

Fruit trees in containers will also be in blossom later in spring. In early spring, sow annuals like

'Angel's Choir' double poppies, which will not disturb the tree roots, around the tree base; or try a more lightweight annual climber like canary creeper or perhaps annual herbs like coriander or dill. Pollinate fruit trees on balconies.

Overwintered parsley plants will be putting on a mass of bright green new growth and can be picked regularly. If they need company, add some violas from the garden centre and think about sowing some baby blue eyes (*Nemophila insignis*) in autumn. This pretty, low-growing, blue-and-white annual will flower among the parsley foliage the following spring.

Lettuce, chards and round carrots can be planted in growing bags, which are also practical for CCA salad crops, though less elegant than a trough.

Seasonal reminders

This inspiring season is a busy time! Sow and plant new crops and new annuals, and divide perennials. Prune shrubs and plant ornamentals of all kinds. Whether planted from pots or in plugs, vegetables and herbs are important in the all-in-one garden from the day they are set out. Always water them into their new home with a liquid fertilizer.

In raised beds in particular, a row of seedlings across a 1.2m (4ft) bed seems to have a more appealing presence than in a larger, less well-defined border. Make sure rows are straight (if you need them to be straight) and use a string stretched across between two canes, or your rake handle laid across the bed, as a

LEFT: *The symmetry of these straight rows of seedlings across this brick-edged bed make a pretty picture with a border of flowers behind.*

RIGHT: *'Benenden Blue' is an unusually neat variety of rosemary with dark leaves and bright blue flowers, ideal for smaller gardens or in containers.*

FAR RIGHT: *Bushy rosemary and flowering thyme are easily picked, while, behind, spring colour comes from tulips and a variegated miscanthus.*

guide. If you need seedlings in a curve or series of curves, mark out the line with some very dry sand (dried in the microwave or the oven, if necessary). Pour the sand from a wine bottle or other container.

Less hardy vegetables can be sown without protection in late spring, but if a cold frame, cold greenhouse or even a cosy porch is available they can be started sooner. Sow French beans and runner beans two to a pot and thin to one. Also sow sweetcorn and the fat (but poisonous) seeds of the castor oil plant, which develops large, maple-like leaves and is an excellent summer partner. Tomatoes, peppers and aubergines need more warmth – a window-sill or propagator is suitable. Tomato and pepper plants are available by mail order and can be potted up and grown on before going outside after the last frost.

Courgettes and marrows can also be sown in late spring. Push pairs of their flat seeds on their edges into pots of moist compost and keep them warm. Those indispensable annual climbers, the morning glories, can be raised in the same way, but canary creeper is tougher and needs less heat. Twine these annuals through fruit trees and bushes in summer.

Cane fruit is growing strongly now, and the new shoots of blackberries and tayberries in particular need attention. Tie them in vertically as they grow but keep them away from the older canes, which will be flowering soon.

Graham's top spring flower and foliage partners for food plants
- *Alchemilla* (lady's mantle)
- Clematis
- Daffodils and other spring bulbs
- Forget-me-nots
- Hardy geraniums
- Heucheras
- Hostas
- Nigella (overwintered)
- Tulips
- Violas

LEFT: *This mixed planting of chives, oregano and rosemary in a neatly edged bed provides an attractive contrast of both colour and form.*

RIGHT: *Curly parsley is an invaluable all-in-one garden plant and looks especially good planted with violas or other seasonal flowers, such as forget-me-nots.*

Summer in the all-in-one garden

Throughout summer, the all-in-one garden is at its most productive, its most colourful and sometimes at its most startling. When those big, sky blue morning glories open their silky trumpets over your purple Brussels sprouts, then you know your all-in-one garden is coming along nicely.

Structure

A garden's basic structure is overwhelmed by planting at this time of year as perennials lean over neat box hedges and impede the necessary clipping late in the season. Paths need weeding, although stray seedlings of dill, coriander and California poppies can be left.

This is when those painstakingly stained boards or low, painted walls around raised beds repay the effort. They form part of the delightful contrasts of colour and texture as leaves overhang their sharp, straight edges. The most appealing combinations are created when the line of colour is broken by foliage from beets, coloured chards, lettuces, mizuna greens, bushy runner beans, chives, parsley, heuchera and spare bedding plants slotted in here and there.

Walls and fences

Here the apples and pears provide a rich green background for old-fashioned sweet peas, which were sown the previous autumn and are now flowering cheerfully. You will need a little space in front of the fruit to pick or dead-head them, as the border is becoming crowded. The Brussels sprouts are filling out

and making their presence felt more every day, and behind them blue delphinium spires are striking through vertically and are buoyed by clouds of feathery green fennel alongside.

Raspberries are dripping off the canes and may not even make it to the kitchen as the gluttonous gardener – and the kids – sample just another to confirm that fine juicy flavour. They are in their prime as vertical accents in rows or tied to posts in the border, with a few ubiquitous canary creepers using them for support. Blackberries and tayberries are flowering in early summer and in front, foxgloves make an appealing vertical accent against the horizontally trained branches of these cane fruits. At the base, hardy geraniums add colour and smother weeds, or strawberries start to ripen from early summer and, depending on the variety, just keep coming for weeks.

Fruit trees

While the fruit on walls is providing more background than colour, free-standing trees are dripping with crops in the form of plums and cherries and also serving as supports for climbers. On a large scale, the well-shaped yellow flowers of the vigorous *Clematis* 'Bill MacKenzie' are colouring old apple trees, while smaller trees host more manageable clematis in the form of *C. viticella* varieties.

Apart from winter, when the developing branch structure of currants trained on walls can be

This trellis tower supports fragrant sweet peas; as they fade, runner beans will take over, opening their scarlet flowers followed by long pods.

attractive, this is the only season when currants – redcurrants in particular – have appeal as their strings of sparkling red beads catch the sunlight and your attention. The fruits are especially visible when grown in high raised beds or large containers, which allow a view into the plant rather than down on it when the leaves tend to hide everything. Less agile gardeners will appreciate high, brick-built raised beds, which can also look very effective with strawberries and perhaps some clumps of early daffodils.

Beds and borders

In summer, colour is everywhere in the borders. The beans are running up their towers and flowering and fruiting heartily, and are perhaps mixed with flowering climbers such as sweet peas, nasturtiums or morning glories. Pick the bean pods regularly to ensure they keep coming. Dwarf runners, especially 'Hestia' with its large, red-and-white flowers, are delightful with summer violas or the slightly domed white heads of invaluable – and undeservedly neglected – garlic chives. Rugosa roses at the back of the border are in bloom in purple, pink or white.

Red cabbage is starting to expand, and an early sowing may begin to heart up. This cabbage is especially effective when combined with the yellow leaves and magenta flowers of *Geranium* 'Ann Folkard' running underneath. Conveniently, this variety does not root as it spreads, enabling the cabbage to have access to all the moisture. Magenta trailing petunias, or

perhaps in a softer pastel pink, planted as groundcover will do a similar job, as will yellow or cherry red calibrachoa. Yellow-leaved, hardy tradescantia is a more compact option. The bold upright swords of irises or, on a larger scale, phormiums also look good against the broad rosettes of the cabbage.

Lupins make dramatic flowering partners with a clump of feathery carrots. When the flowers are over, plants can be cut back hard and watered well to encourage a fresh crop of handsome leaves.

When purple Brussels sprouts are intermingled with the wiry, determinedly vertical stems of *Verbena bonariensis* topped with purple flowerheads, a striking mix of contrast in form and harmony in colour is created in the bed or border.

Upright sweetcorn also makes a bold presence in summer displays. The need for it to be grown in blocks, rather than in rows, to facilitate wind pollination allows it to fit nicely in a border. When planted from pots in late spring, sweetcorn growth is rapid. Bold foliage crops like rhubarb or red chard – or perhaps red lettuce as a shorter term intermingler – make an excellent partner.

Sweetcorn presents the all-in-one gardener with a dilemma. The best corn makes an impressive plant and will crop well, but there are also ornamental varieties of sweetcorn. These have leaves brightly striped in white and pink, which look even more dramatic than the plain green-leaved variety, but they rarely produce a worthwhile crop.

The broad, fingered foliage of lupins, with their scarlet spikes, is attractively fronted by the feathery foliage of carrots while dark-leaved dahlias provide additional contrast.

Raised beds

For sheer productivity, a bush tomato in a traditional, low raised bed will provide a prodigious crop. The tangle of growth makes good groundcover, yet each plant needs plenty of space. Two plants set to spread across the bed – a yellow-fruited variety at one point and a red variety further along – will certainly give a heavy crop. Mid-sized, bushy French marigolds will burst through the tangle effectively, while leeks will make a bold foliage contrast, as will a row of tall calendulas, in orange and yellow shades, for cutting.

Onions look dramatic with their clusters of fat tubular leaves erect above, preferably, glistening red bulbs. They are best sited at the end of the bed, furthest from your view, so that red-leaved beet alongside seems right up close from a distance – onions dislike being too crowded. Onions are ready to eat only when their tops fall – never force this.

The profusion of salads can also be impressive if lettuce of all kinds have been sown in short rows. The range in itself makes an attractive picture, especially with neat basket plants like trailing antirrhinums planted at the edge, between the lettuce rows, to spill over the boards. The lettuce can be interspersed with spring onions, a seed bed of leeks if you prefer to sow them outside, or a row of variegated sedges for posies.

Dwarf beans are flowering and cropping furiously, and they create quite a show with spring-sown cut flowers such as dwarf cosmos, which may grow rather taller than 'dwarf' in the richness of a raised bed, or blue-and-white, bicoloured *Salvia farinacea* 'Strata', which is useful for cutting.

The vegetable tapestry

The intricate tapestry of CCA salad leaves is in a constant state of looking wonderful, because it is being cut regularly, resprouting, being cut again and being sown afresh. Sow CCA crops wherever space allows, but especially around and among upright summer annuals like nigella, geraniums and osteospermums, where they make an attractive background. If sown when these flowering annuals go in, there will be time to take a few cuts before the foliage above closes over. This is the time to experiment with new flavours, by trying a different mixture or a new single variety or by adding a few seeds of a herb – coriander, for example – to see how you like the flavour.

Having plenty of salad leaves ready for picking is a great way of involving dinner guests in helping prepare a meal. Just give them a bowl and a pair of kitchen scissors and tell them to snip away.

Mediterranean herbs

In high summer, in a hot, sheltered corner of the all-in-one garden, the aroma rising from herbs as their essential oils vaporize in the heat can take you right back to your Mediterranean holidays. A tricolor salad – with home-grown tomatoes and basil, of course – in the shade of an overhead vine is an ideal lunch. And you just have to reach upwards for the dessert.

Cistus will be flowering among the thymes, sages and rosemary, while annuals like corn marigolds and scarlet pimpernel will still be blooming; allow some seedheads to develop to provide seedlings for next year. The warmth brings coriander to flower early, while heat and good drainage enhances the flavour. Most of the bulbs have finished flowering, and their dead foliage will need tidying away.

The fig on the wall is magnificent as its fat stems develop and are hung with those huge Adam-and-Eve leaves – just reach for a different dessert. The white cup-and-saucer vine twining through it, enjoying the same warm conditions, is starting to repay its early start on the window-sill.

Also on the wall, the rich blue foamy clouds of ceanothus make a harmonious background for big, blue-leaved euphorbias and silvery cardoons, with self-sown wild antirrhinums below often behaving as perennials in the gravel.

Around the patio and deck

Slightly tender plants and those that appreciate the extra warmth that is a feature of sheltered patios are now coming into their own. The protection from wind and the warmth retained in all that brickwork or paving creates a very cosy microclimate.

Tomatoes are doing well and tall yellow cherry tomatoes tied to their canes alongside tall single striped French marigolds are looking wonderful, especially with bronze-leaved heucheras at the base.

Exotic abutilons, with their big peachy bells, swing over clumps of red-leaved beetroot and flower more prolifically in this sheltered area.

Aubergines, in particular, benefit from warmth, and their glossy fruits will be abundant in rich soil, perhaps in slightly raised beds and with a seep hose watering system. Their broad foliage makes a good contrast with the slender leaves of agapanthus, which appreciate the same conditions.

On the fence, the lablab beans, with their vinous leaves, purplish flowers and shiny flat pods, are falling forward and twining into the orange cannas. The neat and slender rosemary leaves on upright stems contrast with the broad paddles of the canna and the felted silver of plectranthus. Peaches trained on the wall are fruiting and the melon red thunbergias, which appreciate the warmth more than other varieties, look especially pretty twined into them.

Containers

Three tasks dominate for summer containers: watering and feeding; dead-heading flowers and picking crops; and simply enjoying the spectacle.

Containers large and small are at their most colourful and productive in summer. They may be planted with a specimen of 'Tricolor' sage or scarlet bedding geraniums that have been moved into part of the garden where a little extra colour is needed. The lemon tree may be dripping with fruits ready for the after-work gin and tonic, and an urn may be looking

Tomatoes and bright geraniums back rows of chard and cabbage; the foliage of the newly planted chard will soon fill out and cover the bare soil.

triumphant with its banana tree, fiery-looking coleus and fiery-tasting chilli pepper.

For basil, shelter and warm nights can make the difference between productive plants and embarrassing ones. When grown in pots, basil can be placed in exactly the right situation and moved into the cosiest corner as the sun drops in the sky late in the season. An ideal companion for purple basil is variegated tulbaghia, with its mild onion flavour and edible flowers. For something similar, but hardier, try variegated agapanthus, even though it is purely ornamental.

Nectarines, apricots and peaches, as well as hardier container fruits like plums, are cropping well, but do keep an eye on their state of ripeness as the birds may be doing the same. Treat neighbours to the task during holidays – if nothing else to prevent plum juice from staining the deck – and make sure they do the watering at the same time. Trim specimen evergreens, like bay trees, to smarten them up for winter.

Seasonal reminders

This is peak season for cropping and replacing and for weeding and watering. Regular picking of podded plants – peas and beans – is essential to keep them coming, and if you leave your CCA crops too long their tasty sweetness will decline and some may start to stretch uncomfortably. Early sowings of salads are fading and can be removed, but try to replace them with a different type or at least a different colour. All sorts of other short-term crops may need another sowing, although some, like pak choi, are unhappy in the height of a hot summer.

Climbers of all kinds need tying in, both to ensure that they cover their required area and to help support the crop. Everything from clematis and climbing roses to cucumbers and lablab beans will probably need attention. To prevent the long summer wands on cane fruits from breaking, they must be tied in regularly.

Dead-head or pick flowers of all kinds and take the sideshoots off tall tomatoes to concentrate their energy into fruits rather than more leafy growth.

RIGHT: *A screen of scarlet-flowered runner beans backs this fiery grouping of achilleas, crocosmias, dahlias, goldenrods and calendulas, with low red-flushed apples in between to create a brilliant flower-and-food combination.*

LEFT: *This bushy, small leaved basil makes an attractive combination with the broad-leaved variegated plectranthus.*

Trained apples, indeed preferably all apples, need summer pruning to help keep them compact and to encourage generous cropping.

Continue to weed regularly – not so much by setting time aside for a weeding session, though that may prove necessary – but more by simply pulling out any weed you happen to spot as you enjoy the garden. If you set an example when you are in the garden with a friend, perhaps they will copy you.

This is the top time for watering. If you have a drip- or seep-hose system set up there will not be too many watering cans to haul about the garden, except when feeding the plants. But do check that timers are actually doing their job – sometimes they jam.

Graham's top summer flower and foliage partners for food plants

- Achillea
- Canary creeper
- Clematis
- Coleus
- Cosmos
- Hardy geraniums
- Heuchera
- Impatiens
- Morning glory
- Sweet peas

Autumn in the all-in-one garden

The traditional harvest season sees the all-in-one garden laden with crops and looking rich and colourful. Fruits of all kinds, from apples to pumpkins, are ripening, while asters and chrysanthemums are clothed in their autumnal richness. Some crops are coming to the end of their season. Borders wait to be tidied and the compost heap begins to overflow with what will be next year's garden compost.

Structure

In early autumn the structure of the all-in-one garden is at its least obvious, yet by the end of autumn it is at its most clear. In contrast to the softening achieved by lavish foliage earlier in the year, the basic structure is now revealed again in its solidity and clean line, as leaves and dead stems are cleared away. While the scattering of fallen leaves on hedges and paths is comforting and atmospheric, foliage should be swept and gathered before the frosts and snow; make it into a pile of its own as a mulch and soil improver for choice woodland plants.

Walls and fences

On walls and fences, pick apples and other fruits at their peak, then eat or store them. Wall shrubs and climbers, kiwi fruit or clematis, are at the stage when they boast their most voluminous growth of the year. Autumn rains and gales can bring them down, and a temporary repair may be necessary as you pick the fruit or admire the flowers. Melons and grapes are weighed down with fruit in early autumn, so the plants need looking after carefully.

Cut out all canes that have fruited from blackberry and tayberry plants, and train the new canes along their wires before they become too stiff and likely to break; tie them in with soft twine. Raspberries need similar treatment, but as the canes are short enough not to have to bend when tied to the support wires the timing is less critical.

Fruit trees

After the harvest and the late-summer training, fruit trees need little attention. Some may be producing attractive autumn colour, which is lovely with autumn sedums, schizostylis, asters and chrysanthemums.

Crab apples will often retain their fruit for months, dominating the garden into winter – the red-fruited varieties often lasting the longest. Theoretically, these should go to make jelly, but they are such a treat when set against a clear blue winter sky that leaving them is a good option. Eventually the birds will find them irresistible.

Beds and borders

Some crops are at their peak, some are fading, while others are just coming into their stride. The consistency and continuity of your cropping into autumn will depend on the extent to which you kept up with successional sowing on a variety of vegetables. Salad plants can still be producing during autumn, but

A row of red dahlias and a few white cosmos bring colour to the intriguing foliage of the maincrop carrots and salsify.

only if you made some further timely sowings after the main spring sowing season.

Cropping of purple-podded peas will have tailed off. You may even have cut down the plants and planted salads in their place to make use of the nitrogen that is released by their rotting roots. But if you made another sowing in early summer and the summer was not so hot as to discourage good growth, you will have more peas now.

Broad beans will be over, although seed of some varieties can be sown in autumn for an early crop next year. Dwarf French beans will still be lifting their purple pods over their foliage if you sowed late and kept the plants moist. And while the sweet peas that mingled with the runner beans will probably have faded away, flowers and bean pods will still be coming from a late spring sowing if you have picked regularly. From a second sowing, they will be prolific. If you planted morning glory to twine among the beans, they will both be moving into a stage when growth slows and flowering becomes concentrated towards the ends of the shoots. The late flowers on scarlet runner beans can be really dramatic.

Pumpkins and so many of their relations are ripening well. It is a good idea to snip off some of the foliage to expose fruits to the sun and help them on their way to maturity. Cut modest-sized orange pumpkins – 30cm (1ft) or so across – and arrange them in groups on steps or in the front of borders with autumn flowers behind.

Cut back hard perennials of all kinds, be they artichokes or rhubarb, phlox or delphiniums. Their old growth can augment the compost heap. Work with care, because late flowers, vegetables and fruits may be still at their best. Some plants, such as perennial grasses, which retain an attractive structure throughout the winter, can be left until spring before yielding to the secateurs.

Raised beds

The sequence of sow or plant–harvest–remove–sow or plant continues for both food and flowers in raised beds. Although resowing crops becomes less of an option, there are winter and next spring to consider.

The technique of harvesting both flowers and food can change a little as the season rolls on. Rows of lettuce, parsley, cornflowers, annual chrysanthemums and chards, where you have been picking a few leaves or a few flowers from each plant, can be cut completely if they are not to make a contribution during winter. Spring-sown chard plants can be pulled whole, and Eggs Florentine can go on the menu for your next supper party. Later sowings will happily provide occasional pickings in cold weather and then surge into growth in spring.

Leeks will be bulking up and looking dramatic against late-sown red cabbage or, nestling at their feet, mottled heucheras, which are invaluable for providing foliage for dainty arrangements at table settings right through winter. They go well with snowdrops.

Autumn colour tones combine red cabbage and leeks with red orache and other fading annuals in an attractive end-of-the-season display.

Bushy tomatoes are producing fruits in a rush, and slugs and birds may be paying them too close attention; the vigorous low and bushy types may produce the best crops but they are more vulnerable. Hay or straw from the pet shop spread underneath helps as a deterrent. Frost will soon stop everything in its tracks, so pick all tomatoes as winter approaches. If you have a glut, make tomato soup and freeze it. Green tomatoes can be ripened by the traditional method of laying them out, so they do not touch each other, on a cloth in a kitchen drawer with a banana. (The banana gives off ethylene, which encourages the tomatoes to ripen.) The stems and leaves can go on the compost heap.

Sow salad onions in early autumn for spring use. Their tight, upright shapes will look well in winter. Garlic and those onion sets specifically intended for autumn planting can also go in, as can winter-sown lettuce. Rows of the hardier cut-flower annuals, especially cornflowers and nigella, will make much larger plants when sown in early autumn.

The vegetable tapestry
The growth of CCA salads is so rapid and the soil is so warm that sowings in early autumn may crop twice, depending on the season and climate. However, unless a protected environment is available – like a cold greenhouse, which tends to be neglected and underused in winter – late autumn sees a break in salad production until spring.

Mediterranean herbs
The warmth and sun of a sheltered site help herbs to ripen well and harden off for winter. By hardening their wood, sages, rosemaries and even twiggy little thymes can better tolerate winter frost. But the shoots can still be cut or pinched for kitchen use. Indeed the soft tips are often the parts that suffer most in winter so pick them now.

Autumn is also tidy-up time. Pull out annual herbs that have begun to look ragged and so create more compost. Cut back perennials when their seedheads have lost their charm, and if necessary give artichokes and cardoons some winter protection with a mound of gravel or a layer of straw.

Around the patio and deck
Clear-out-and-crop time is here, with cannas, bananas and dahlias first at their peak and then needing winter protection, either in the garage or a cold greenhouse. Their blackening by frost is the sign that they require shelter. Cut off the tops and take them to the compost heap, along with all the summer annuals and bedding plants. Tender summer vegetables will also need to be removed (*see* Containers, right). This creates space, which is fortunate as this is bulb planting time. Hardy bulbs, which increase well and can emerge through shorter term crops, can go in now. Daffodils – increasingly available in pinks as well as yellow, orange and white – should be priorities along with smaller bulbs like crocuses and dark blue and ice blue scillas.

This terracotta pot of ruby chard and scarlet petunias creates a focal point in this autumn border planted with purple sage and yellow rudbeckias.

Radicchio is coming into its own and teams up well with the blue-grey leaves of autumn sedums. Butterflies are stocking up on nectar from the pink or white flowers before migration or hibernation. By spring, the radicchio should still be in good condition, having benefited from a little overwinter shelter, and will look good with dark blue scillas.

Chards too retain their colour and shape well with a little protection. Pick them over regularly as summer slides into winter. Evergreen perennials, like bergenias and heucheras as well as choice hellebores, are good companions right through into late winter when the bulbs join them. Purple mustard is developing well and will also stand attractively right through the cold weather when it really shines.

Containers

There comes a point when feeding and watering tomatoes, aubergines and peppers in containers become a waste of time. All they will do is stand still – neither growing nor developing more fruits – so pick the last fruits, use them, remove the old plants to the compost heap and apply the potting compost itself as mulch on to borders. Be sure to break up the old compost with a hand fork so it is not lying in lumps.

All temporary plantings – vegetables or summer flowers – can come out now and the compost used as mulch. Winter and spring planting schemes can take over. Move evergreens in containers – herbs, shrubs or perennials – to where they will be more prominent so they stand out in the more subdued situation.

Citrus trees in containers will now need to be given a little protection against frost damage.

It is a good idea to plant evergreens – either as specimens or in groups – in the containers from which summer plants have been removed. They can remain there until spring, when they can come out and be planted in the soil. Alternatively, they can be left to develop into more permanent container specimens.

Temporary evergreen plantings for winter and spring will never attain the imposing stature of summer plantings, so smaller containers are more appropriate. Choose combinations of chards, purple mustard, parsley, sage, endive, even late-sown red cabbage, with pansies and violas, wallflowers, polyanthus, tulips and other spring bulbs.

Seasonal reminders

Two tasks dominate: clearing up and preparing for winter; and sowing and planting for spring. Autumn is the season for filling the compost bin with the remains of summer crops, such as cane fruit prunings, which may be stiff enough to provide that vital supporting network at the base that allows air access. Later, compost all the cut stems of perennials and annuals pulled from beds, borders and containers. This is when the organic matter that goes under new fruit trees and new shrubs is created.

Mulching is sometimes done in autumn and sometimes in spring – the timing depends on the material available and the plants among which the mulch is to be spread. A fine mulch, always the best – composted bark perhaps – can be spread at any time among perennials that are evergreen or have not died down, because its crumbly structure allows it to be worked among plants. Even if it is fairly mature, farmyard manure can be lumpy and therefore more difficult to work around evergreen plants like bergenias. It is perhaps best reserved for those few areas of the all-in-one garden where perennials are less crowded; you can also use it when planting tree and cane fruits. Late autumn is the best time to plant fruit trees and ornamental deciduous trees, as well as raspberries and other fruits.

Dealing with fallen leaves is important as they can smother overwintering plantings and set off rots. A hand fork will help extricate them from tightly planted situations. If there are few groundcovering perennials, move old leaves under trees, shrubs and fruit; otherwise, store them in their own leaf litter heap.

Graham's top autumn flower and foliage partners for food plants

- Asters
- Autumn-colouring shrubs
- Chrysanthemums
- Clematis
- Heucheras
- Ornamental grasses
- Sedums
- Violas and pansies

As these hydrangea flowers fade into the red and russet tones of autumn, the 'Cox's Orange Pippin' apples are ripening well, surrounded by evergreen euonymus and silver cinerarias.

Winter in the all-in-one garden

The traditional vegetable plot is not always the most interesting part of the winter garden. Large areas will have been left roughly dug for the frost to work on the soil. While some plants will be making their presence felt, many will be looking a little the worse for wear. However, in the all-in-one garden things are different because you choose only those plants that are convincing contributors to the winter scene and you grow them with other plants that are naturally at their peak at this time of year.

There is less growth and less foliage everywhere in the garden in winter, but the advantage of this situation is that it emphasizes the structure in the all-in-one garden, especially after a dusting of snow or a silvering of hoarfrost.

Structure

The layout of low evergreen hedges which mark out the structure of the garden – be they box, sage or germander – is now highlighted along with the layout of paths. Variegated box, so good bordering red-leaved lettuce in summer, now reveals its winter texture. This is the time of year when your wobbly hedge planting line, uneven clipping, unbalanced layout or the uneven pattern in your brick paving is revealed. It may also be the period when poor or puddled paths actually discourage you from venturing out to pick kales or chards.

Winter is also the season when the extra time spent ensuringe that the board fence is truly upright proves really worthwhile, when the additional expense of a woven hazel screen is justified in the creation not only of a barrier but also of an attractive feature in itself, and when choosing the right stain for those boards proves to be time well spent. For in winter, all is revealed. And this includes the bold and upright shapes of apple trees trained into slender rockets – under various trade names including Ballerina™ and Minarette – punctuating the garden with exclamations and with those trained horizontally just above ground, the step-over trees.

Use the winter revelations to plan indoors on paper what structures and other details require attention. Take pictures now to record what needs changing or amending, removing or adding. Planning and dreaming are part of winter fireside reflections.

Walls and fences

On walls or fences, tiers of espaliered apples, pears or currants – year by year becoming more gnarled – make an attractive restful pattern and also reveal old birds' nests lodged in the forks of the branches. At their base, overwintered sweet peas from an autumn sowing continue to send down their roots in mild spells. These roots will support a long flowering season to follow the fruit flowers early in summer.

Winter wall shrubs and climbers like the daintily spotted winter clematis (*C. cirrhosa*), fragrant *Acacia dealbata* and *Daphne bholua* (with its usefully upright habit) and dependable evergreen garrya are in their

Winter plants like leeks, red cabbage, curly kale and this ornamental kale have a bold structure and strong colouring which is even more striking when the leaves are edged with early morning frost.

prime. Later these plants will host purple-podded peas and beans or possibly lablab beans.

Fruit trees

A specimen crab apple, its bright red fruits still untouched by birds and gleaming in the sunlight, stands out against a clear blue sky or, in a container perhaps, is set against the dark green of a conifer hedge. On fences and walls, and in tubs, the buds of peaches and other fruit trees are fattening. The birds may have their eye on them, so protect buds from birds and frost with fleece, even though it is not aesthetically pleasing. Fine black netting will keep off the birds and is almost invisible but is not frostproof.

Peaches may also need pollination. When these trees are under fleece the bees cannot reach their flowers, if indeed the bees are around at the time of early flowerers. The way to fertilize them, therefore, is to flutter a basic-grade artist's paint brush in the centre of each flower.

The scarlet fruits of 'Red Sentinel' crab apples often last well right through the winter providing a final feast for the birds when they need it most.

Beds and borders

Although this is hardly peak season in beds and borders, combining flowers and food is still worthwhile in the all-in-one garden. The solid heads of purple curly kale reveal an intricate pattern of fine leaves. Like purple curly parsley when glistening with morning frost, it seems a pity to pick the kale. The white-veined leaves of wintergreen arum (*A. italicum*), like slender arrowheads, make a bold contrast at the base of the kale, where daffodils are emerging too in a hint of the dramatic colour combination to come.

Mature evergreen clumps, like small shrubs, of evergreen bear's foot hellebores, *H. foetidus*, are coming into flower with snowdrops round the base bobbing daintily; radicchio or red mustard will pick up the reddish edging in the hellebore flowers.

Even if borders are predominantly bare, with summer perennials and summer vegetables not in view, a pattern of leeks running through the border in a slender line, will add to the structure in a series of gentle curves, in a zigzag or in a triangular block where the leaves of the frontal plants arch over the box edging.

Raised beds

In raised beds, the leaves of the last few red cabbages – left a little too long, perhaps – or purple mustards hang over the edge of boards stained in pale teal and reveal a pretty colour combination. The bold, upright stems of two rows of overwintered broad beans, for early flowers and pods, make a stark contrast. A rarely indulged winter treat is a posy of snowdrops on the table. Plant a vigorous named variety, like *Galanthus* 'Magnet' or *G.* 'S. Arnott', in a row across your bed. Mark the spot, and in late summer or early autumn plant a row of purple mustards alongside. In a few years there will be sufficient snowdrops to pick for posies and to cheer the winter garden. In another row red chicory holds it colour well, with the jagged rosettes of mizuna greens. A couple of purple Brussels sprouts stand out dramatically, and those blue leeks are ideal companions alongside.

The roots of plants in raised beds are more susceptible than plants in borders to severe freezes, thaws and refreezing, so mulch perennial plants heavily.

Mediterranean herbs

Among the Mediterranean herbs, the upright growth of *Rosmarinus officinalis* 'Miss Jessopp's Upright' makes a striking accent, especially on a frosty morning. It may even produce a few flowers if nestled cosily close to a wall, perhaps alongside the pretty little evergreen *Coronilla glauca* with its yellow, honey-scented pea-flowers. Brush any snow from these and other evergreens to avoid it weighing down their branches and ruining the shape.

Vine branches trained on the wall are year by year becoming endearingly craggier. The outline of the fat fig branches is especially striking. Winter iris should be blooming well, while the silver rosettes of horned poppy hug the gravel around the textured evergreen leaves of purple sage.

Frost brings a new look and satisfying atmosphere to these box balls and cabbages, set off by well swept, neat brick paths.

Around the patio and deck

Quite how much is happening on your patio or deck – both in terms of cropping and colour – often depends on how protected and sheltered it is and how much of a sun trap. In a cosy corner, rosemary will flower in winter, especially *Rosmarinus officinalis* 'Tuscan Blue'. Chards can be picked right through, and although they can look limp after a hard frost they usually perk up. The white- and orange-stemmed varieties can look spectacular with red-leaved bergenias (or purple mustard). Alongside them, violas will be flowering, as well as the earliest bulbs.

Indeed many shrubs, perennials and bulbs and a few winter bedding plants can bring colour to the patio and deck when little else is making the effort. Many plants, like leeks and sprouts, are not ideal in and around the deck and patio, so in winter ornamentals and evergreen herbs in pots are to be valued. In a frost pocket the situation will be more bleak.

Containers

In the all-in-one garden winter is more than a season of digging and cosying up to the fire. There is beauty in such a garden and there is even still food to pick for the kitchen.

At the front door, in elegant square boxes or more rustic terracotta pots, a pair of tall pyramidal bay trees flanks the door. These 'practical' Christmas trees can be decorated with fairy lights each year. To keep them neatly shaped they need regular watering, an

Red curly kale is a tough plant which retains its colour all winter and will survive a frosty night.

occasional liquid feed and a little clipping if demand from the kitchen is slow. Early crocuses will open around the base at winter's end in this sheltered spot. In summer they are overplanted with white lobelia.

In the porch, or on the patio, a terracotta pot featuring a single rosemary plant with variegated thyme around the edges makes a stylish feature. The thymes are interplanted with a few winter violas (not pansies, whose flowers are too large to combine well with the delicate herb foliage). Make sure the pot is lifted off the soil to allow free drainage and turn it a little every week so that plants are evenly exposed to light.

Seasonal reminders

Winter is the season for preparing new beds and revitalizing old ones. Digging can be a crippling business, even though it does have the beneficial effect of working off the effects of too many holiday parties. Years later, even healthy youngsters may feel the effects of digging overenthusiastically in their prime. Just two separate half hours a day, most weekends for a month or two, will see a job done painlessly which some people might tackle in one long weekend at the last minute as spring approaches and thus risk injury.

This is the season to cut autumn-fruiting raspberries right back to the ground. Then mulch

Hellebores are essential winter-flowering plants whose bold summer foliage makes a striking edging long after the flowers themselves are over.

them, along with other soft fruit, taking care not to smother perennials. Work the mulch around strawberries planted at the base. Grapes need pruning in early or midwinter, before the sap starts to move and the cuts bleed. To keep apples neat in growth and productive, cut back all sideshoots to between three and six buds and the main shoot by at least a quarter.

The first lettuces and peas and a wide range of other crops, and hardy annuals, can be sown in a cold greenhouse in late winter. If these are moved outside in early spring you will have a flying start with both flowers and food.

If the extra choice of varieties available in mail order catalogues appeals, make your selections and place orders from the leisurely comfort of the early-winter fireside rather than in the last-minute rush of the spring sowing season, when the best varieties may have sold out.

Graham's top winter flower and foliage partners for food plants
- Arums
- Bergenias
- Crocus
- Garrya
- Hellebores
- Snowdrops
- Winter aconites

04 | Plant Guide

All-in-one gardeners are now better served than ever before. All the features they look for, especially if space is limited, are appearing in more and more varieties. This makes food plants more attractive in their own right and also better companions for flowering plants.

Foliage, flowers and even fruits in interesting colours are combined with other invaluable factors, such as high yield, long season, good flavour, pest and disease resistance and modest size. The best garden centres now stock a wider selection of these plants than ever before, and many mail order companies are also offering all-in-one plants and seeds, so actually finding them is not usually an issue.

Do keep in mind that some food plants are, frankly, not especially attractive and so not every plant in the catalogue is discussed here.

Wonderful effects can be created by planting rows of cut flowers, like these gaillardias and celosias, with bold vegetables such as Brussels sprouts.

Fruit

Fruit provides some of the most tempting tastes in the all-in-one garden. It is also an invaluable presence with trees and bushes providing structure all through the seasons. Most fruits have two seasons of colour: spring flowers are followed by summer or autumn fruits. Some gardeners worry about factors that rarely arise with other plants – rootstocks, special pruning techniques and pollination – yet modern varieties have taken much of the mystery out of fruit growing and it is easier to cultivate than ever.

Tree fruit

Tree fruit is unexpectedly useful in the all-in-one garden, both as a multi-season feature in its own right and as a partner with other food and flowering plants. The word 'tree' implies something uncomfortably large, yet when fruit trees are grown in containers,

which help keep otherwise vigorous plants like plums to a manageable size, they make excellent small specimens. Against walls, fences and on horizontal wires, fruit can be trained as a cordon (a single angled stem), as an espalier (a series of horizontal stems), as a fan (stems radiating from the base) and as U or double-U (two or four vertical stems trained from a single short basal stem). All can be kept small enough that they are easy to look after.

Almost all fruit trees consist of two parts. The variety, by which the plant is known and that produces the crop, is grafted on to a rootstock, known by a name or code, which governs the size and vigour of the tree. Unless you buy from a specialist fruit grower, most fruit is sold grafted on to rootstocks that keep the plants relatively small and encourage early fruiting. When you are buying, look for a well-branched tree or bush with branches that are distributed evenly around the main stem.

When planting, make sure that the bulge at the base of the stem, where the two parts meet, is just above the ground. It is important to tie the young tree securely to a short, stout stake until its roots have become well established, though this is less necessary in a container sited in a sheltered position.

Only the briefest pruning notes are given here; check the specific requirements of each type of fruit.

Many fruit crops require two different varieties for cross-pollination and thus to produce fruit, so you may need to have two trees, of different varieties. One

'Cox's Orange Pippin' makes an excellent container fruit that produces a good crop if it is kept watered and fed regularly.

useful development in recent years has been the arrival of varieties that set fruit all alone. These are ideal in the all-in-one garden, where variety is one of the keys to all-season cropping and colour.

There are two approaches to companions for fruit trees. One is to plant climbers at the tree base and use the trunk as support; this often works especially well as the climbers usually bloom between the tree's flowering and cropping periods. The other approach is to plant annuals or perennials around the base or alongside the tree. Shallow-rooted varieties are ideal as they compete less with the roots of the tree.

Apples

All apples have at least two seasons during which they contribute colour to the garden: in spring the flurry of white or blushed flowers is delightful and later there are the fruits. But for all-in-one gardeners other factors are also important, particularly shape.

The standard shape, where a broad head is carried on a stem up to 2m (6ft) tall, is the least appealing as the long trunk lifts flowers and fruits so far off the ground that it is difficult to create associations with perennials, annuals, bulbs and shrubs that will not crowd the tree. The fruits are also awkward to pick, and the amount of shade cast can be uncomfortable.

A bush shape is preferable in containers and in borders, but apples also come in a dramatically columnar format, which provides year-round exclamations. They can also be trained on fences and on wires (*see* opposite), and as step-over trees (with long, low, horizontal branches parallel to the ground). Such trained forms are the most appealing in terms of their winter structure.

Graham's top tips for apples

- CHOOSING VARIETIES Select self-fertile varieties, including 'Queen Cox' (the self-fertile version of the nation's favourite apple), 'Goldilocks' and 'Greensleeves'.
- BUYING PLANTS Most trees are grafted on to M9 rootstock, which is ideal for large bush trees, containers, cordons and other trained forms. Look for M27 if you need a smaller bush tree.
- PLANTING Make sure containers are large and deep. Pot-grown and garden trees are happy in full sun, though a little shade from the side

helps prevent containers drying out too quickly. Avoid hot, sunny walls and fences.

- TRAINING AND PRUNING Regularly tie in trees trained flat on a fence, wall or wires. Cut back the new growth of all trees to two or three leaves in summer and to three or four buds in winter. It is worth checking the requirements of specific varieties.
- CARE Regular feeding will encourage heavy crops and resistance to disease.
- GOOD COMPANIONS Guide container-grown, lightweight annual climbers like canary creeper or old-fashioned sweet peas through the tree. Plant fibrous begonias or summer annuals, like poppies, cornflowers or alyssum, at the base. Shallow-rooted perennials like dead nettles and shade-loving hardy geraniums are also good. In the garden, globe artichokes and cottage garden perennials are ideal, as are tulips. Train clematis into large, mature trees.

Crab apples

Although the fruit colour of crab apples is better than dessert apples, their culinary use is largely restricted to preserves. However, these most useful small garden trees and container plants all fruit without a pollinator, and their pollen will fertilize culinary apple trees. They have pretty pink to white spring flowers, fruits that often last well into winter and, sometimes, colourful autumn foliage.

'Evereste' is a neat-growing crab apple that makes a good plant in a small border and that can also be grown in a large container.

Graham's top tips for crabapples

- CHOOSING VARIETIES 'John Downie' is widely available and has the best fruit. 'Golden Hornet' is also good, while 'Evereste', 'Laura' and 'Pom Zai' are all excellent and sometimes available trained as dwarf bushes.
- BUYING PLANTS There is rarely a choice of rootstock for crab apples. Look for well-shaped, well-branched trees.
- PLANTING Grow in a large container or in the open garden in full sun or in the shade of a wall or fence. Can also be trained on a wall or fence.
- TRAINING AND PRUNING Cut new shoots by about half after their first flowering to create a well-branched head, then cut back the new growth to two or three leaves in summer if necessary.
- CARE Keep trained trees tied in securely and watch for pests and diseases.
- GOOD COMPANIONS All make good specimens in their own right; otherwise *see* apples (page 103).

Cherries

Even though they are less dramatic in flower than flowering cherries, fruiting cherries are still delightful in spring, when they bear pretty white flowers followed by juicy flavoursome fruit. You can pick the luscious fruit as soon as it is ripe. Modern varieties remain conveniently compact, and not all need pollination by another tree to be sure of fruit. Cherries are especially suitable for containers, and it is easier to protect the fruit of such smaller trees if birds are a problem. The self-fertile 'Morello' cherry is ideal on a north-facing wall. Its white flowers mature into juicy, deep red fruits in late summer and autumn.

Morello cherries are ideal for training on a north-facing wall and, once established, make a good support for lightweight climbers like canary creeper.

Graham's top tips for cherries

- CHOOSING VARIETIES Select self-fertile types like 'Sunburst', 'Lapins', 'Summer Sun', 'Rubi', 'Self-fertile Stella' and 'Morello'.
- BUYING PLANTS Look for bushy, even crowns and the excellent Gisella 5 rootstock.
- PLANTING Grow in a large container or plant in an open situation, except for 'Morello', which is the top choice for a north-facing wall.
- TRAINING AND PRUNING Keep branches of both container trees and those in an open situation evenly spaced around the crown. In spring, pinch out growing tips, back to five or six leaves. Thin out new shoots of 'Morello' to 10cm (4in) apart to replace fruiting branches.
- CARE Keep trained trees tied in securely and watch for pests and diseases.
- GOOD COMPANIONS Are good as specimens, in containers or the open ground, where the flowers and fruits can make an impact. Try with spring bulbs and tall forget-me-nots .

Figs

These dramatic, sun-loving, foliage plants for borders or containers would be worth growing even if they never produced a fruit. Their big, lobed foliage is so bold and impressive that it is no wonder Adam and Eve wore the leaves for modesty's sake. Fruits, which are carried on vigorous stout branches, ripen well in areas where winters are not too cold as they have the

- TRAINING AND PRUNING Cut back new growth by half in spring to develop a bushy structure. When grown against a wall, spread out the branches about 15cm (6in) apart and tie in each spring; remove any surplus shoots.
- CARE Water in dry spells in summer to help the fruits swell. Move pot-grown plants into a protected area for the winter.
- GOOD COMPANIONS Annual morning glories, Mediterranean herbs and shrubs.

Figs not only feature bold foliage that is impressive by itself, but their luscious fruits are also a wonderful treat.

Grapes

Grapevines combine attractively divided foliage with a luscious crop of black or white grapes, and some even take on pretty autumn tints. They grow well on wires at the back of a sunny border, on a wall, an arbour or trained vertically on a post and are superb for creating a shady nook on the patio. The vines are also easily managed in large tubs and, being relatively drought resistant, are useful for forgetful waterers and dry, sunny gardens.

unusual habit of producing fruits in late summer, which ripen the next year. Figs are drought tolerant.

Graham's top tips for figs
- CHOOSING VARIETIES The most widely available variety, 'Brown Turkey', is also the best in most gardens. The rarer variety 'Bavaria' is unusually hardy.
- BUYING PLANTS Look for good-sized plants with at least two or three branches. Figs are not grafted on to special rootstocks.
- PLANTING Figs crop best when their roots are restricted so are perfect in containers, from 30cm (1ft) upwards. In borders plant against a sunny wall in a big plastic tub (with drainage holes), burying the whole tub. Figs make an excellent backdrop for a Mediterranean herb garden.

Graham's top tips for grapes
- CHOOSING VARIETIES Select varieties listed as suitable for growing outside, rather than in a greenhouse. 'Dornfelda' (black) and 'Phoenix' (white) are good for eating and wine.
- BUYING PLANTS Grapevines are purchased in pots. There is usually no choice of rootstock.
- PLANTING Thrive in plenty of sun either in a

border or a container. Have supports in place before planting.

- TRAINING AND PRUNING Always prune in early winter, otherwise cut shoots may bleed badly. For specific instructions check the plant label or read *Grapes: Indoors and Out* by Harry Baker and Ray Waite.
- CARE Tie in growth as it develops. Water well in dry spells and give liquid feeds to a container-grown vine as the berries develop.
- GOOD COMPANIONS Try annual climbers, wild crocuses, cyclamen and scillas around the base with herbs like coriander and dill. Purple-leaved *Vitis vinifera* 'Purpurea' stands out against a white background and with dark blue or purple clematis, but its fruits aren't as good.

Juicy grapes are not difficult to grow on a warm and sunny wall as long as a few basic pruning practices are followed to maximize crop and keep the vines under control.

Hops

Hops are grown for home brewing, for indoor autumn decoration and to make herbal pillows. Some varieties also have bright buttery yellow leaves, which make them especially useful in the all-in-one garden. The bold, maple-like foliage is carried on vigorous twining plants, which die down in winter. There are also some invaluable new short varieties.

Graham's top tips for hops

- CHOOSING VARIETIES All yellow-leaved varieties are attractive but only female hops carry the decorative flower clusters (the catalogue should indicate which sex is offered).
- BUYING PLANTS Often sold as a 'hill' (a mound of roots), or sometimes in pots; even a small plant will soon make an impressive specimen.
- PLANTING No special requirements, although allow space as the roots can spread.
- TRAINING AND PRUNING Although each year's new shoots are twining, they still need guidance. Cut back to the ground in winter or very early spring, and remove the drying twining shoots from fence supports or shrubs.
- CARE Do not allow to dry out.
- GOOD COMPANIONS Are good trained up trellis, into robust evergreens, like blue spruces, and with blue hardy geraniums around the base.

Peaches, nectarines and apricots

These soft-fruited trees are absolutely ideal in containers on the patio. They can also be trained to grow on wires against a sunny wall. New, smaller, bushier and hardier varieties are easy to grow and flavour-rich. The pink flowers are followed in warm summers by attractive and juicy fruit.

Graham's top tips for stone fruits

- CHOOSING VARIETIES Many modern varieties do not need a pollinator and are disease resistant. In cool winters and cool summers these will thrive; in other climates choose from local sources. Peach 'Saturn' is an unusual flat shape but has masses of flavour and is self-fertile. Apricot 'Petit Muscat' has a wonderful flavour and is self-fertile, while 'Flavourcot' has good flavour and is cold tolerant. The prolific nectarine 'Fantasia' is easy to grow.
- BUYING PLANTS Select young plants, which can be trained for containers or walls, or buy specifically for the shape you have in mind.
- PLANTING Position 30cm (1ft) from a wall or plant in a large container.
- TRAINING AND PRUNING Spread out branches and tie them in evenly against a wall. In a container, little training is required.
- CARE Drape early spring flowers with fleece to protect them from frost. They may also need pollinating by dusting from flower to flower

Peaches are the ideal crop for a sunny wall but it's important to ensure that the plants do not get too dry in the spring and summer as the fruits are developing.

with an artist's paint brush. Make sure trees have plenty of water as the fruits are swelling.
- GOOD COMPANIONS Try sun-loving annual climbers like morning glories and thunbergias.

Pears

These boast pretty spring flowers followed by luscious fruits. Modern advances in pears are a help to the all-in-one gardener and have brought better flavour, good cropping on younger plants and less reliance on a second variety for pollination. Pears are good free-standing trees and also mature into impressive wall specimens.

Graham's top tips for pears

- CHOOSING VARIETIES Select for flavour, though the very tastiest may need a second variety as

Pears are the traditional hardy fruit to be grown on a cool wall and, as the years go by, they will develop an attractive structure of old branches.

a pollinator. 'Concorde' is compact, self-fertile; it fruits on young trees and tastes great. 'Conference' is partially self-fertile, while 'Doyenné du Comice', 'Gourmande', 'Honeygold' and 'Delsanne' are bred for flavour but need a second tree for pollination.

- BUYING PLANTS Are good on a wall or fence, so choose a young plant that can be trained or pay more for one already trained for growing flat. Are less happy in pots than most fruits.
- PLANTING Are best in fertile soil that does not dry out in summer. Keep sheltered from cold winds and early frost.
- TRAINING AND PRUNING Look especially good with the branches trained in horizontal tiers. Cut back to two or three buds in summer.

- CARE Pick the fruits carefully because they bruise very easily.
- GOOD COMPANIONS Plant verticals like foxgloves and delphiniums in front of horizontally-trained wall trees. Train climbers such as clematis or roses into trees planted in the open.

Plums

Clouds of white spring flowers are followed by flavoursome fruits that you can eat straight from the tree. Plums are better grown in containers, which help keep the trees compact, than in the open garden where they can become large and cast too much shade. They are not in the top rank of all-in-one plants because plums are more prone to disease than other fruits and the blossom may be damaged by frosts. They do taste superb, however, so you may like to grow one in a large tub.

Graham's top tips for plums

- CHOOSING VARIETIES Self-fertile 'Victoria' is a heavy cropper and full of flavour; it should be the all-in-one gardener's first choice. The European Mirabelle varieties also have a superb taste.
- BUYING PLANTS Look for bushy, even crowns; there is usually little choice of rootstock.
- PLANTING Grow best in a large tub or half-barrel. Are good on a sunny wall but do not place in early morning sun in spring.

- TRAINING AND PRUNING Try to develop a bushy, compact head. Long shoots can be shortened in summer.
- CARE Treat pests and diseases promptly.
- GOOD COMPANIONS In containers, try with hardy annuals like annual poppies and larkspur and with annual climbers.

Berried fruits

Berried fruits come in three types – cane fruits, bush fruits and strawberies – all of which are easy to grow and appreciate thorough soil preparation. The cane fruits – blackberries, tayberries and raspberries – grow in the same way and are treated similarly. Long canes develop one season and in the next carry pretty white, or sometimes pink, flowers followed by the fruits. These canes should be cut out at the base to make room for new growth. Cane fruits are trained on fences or wires or up vertical poles. Apart from their delicious fruit, they bear attractive flowers and foliage.

Bush fruits comprise currants, gooseberries and blueberries. Most bushes also carry their berries, and their often rather insignificant flowers, on the shoots that grew the previous year. Blueberries are one of the best container-grown fruit bushes. Currants and gooseberries are the least useful soft fruits to the all-in-one gardener, although they are decorative when trained on a wall, where their branch structure becomes a feature, especially in winter. Strawberries are ground cover plants with very attractive flowers.

Blackberries and tayberries

It used to be said that wild blackberries had the best flavour, yet most modern varieties taste wonderful, some have no thorns, and some also feature striking flowers; they bear a huge crop and often have pretty foliage. Tayberries, the hybrid between blackberries and raspberries, are some of the tastiest of all soft fruits and are grown in the same way as blackberries. Both are vigorous and should be trained along a fence or wires. They need regular, straightforward pruning to constrain them and to give the heaviest crop.

Graham's top tips for berries
- CHOOSING VARIETIES Thornless varieties make life so much easier. 'Chester' blackberry is

If you only have room for one cane fruit, trained on a wire, let it be a tayberry for its heavy crop of large, colourful, delicious berries.

outstanding, with its pink flowers and sweet flavour. 'Buckingham' is a fine thornless tayberry. Look out for new varieties as they become available.

- BUYING PLANTS Large plants in pots will establish quickly and often produce a crop in their first year. Plants in small pots are not particularly cost effective.
- PLANTING Grow in a sunny place 2.4–3m (8–10ft) apart against wires trained horizontally at 30–40cm (12–16in) intervals. Tayberries are a little more shade tolerant. Blackberries are not particularly successful in containers, though they will produce a fair crop in a large tub in good light.
- TRAINING AND PRUNING Train new growth together vertically at first, then along the top wire. Cut out old shoots at the base promptly after fruiting and redistribute new growth, tying in along wires.
- CARE Easy, but can be uncomfortably vigorous – and the thorny varieties may be uncomfortable to prune.
- GOOD COMPANIONS The canes and wires set up for these cane fruits can also support annual climbers that are not be too smothering: try old-fashioned sweet peas, canary creeper or morning glory. Strawberries can go below or try groundcovering perennials like hellebores and hardy geraniums or spring bulbs.

Blueberries are among the best of all fruits for containers with dainty white flowers, tasty tart fruits and colourful autumn foliage.

Blueberries

Blueberries are just about the healthiest fruit you can grow – their anti-oxidants are said to protect against heart disease and to slow the ageing process. They are delightful all-in-one plants for containers with their pretty, white, bell-like flowers in spring, bunches of blue berries in summer and fiery autumn colour.

Graham's top tips for blueberries

- CHOOSING VARIETIES Select those that crop in succession to give a long season. The following are all prolific and have large tasty berries. In cropping order they are: 'Earliblue' (midsummer), 'Toro', 'Chandler', 'Herbert' and 'Brigitta' (late summer). There are many more.

Raspberries

This most adaptable and manageable cane fruit bears clusters of pretty white flowers and aromatic tasty berries. Its comparatively short stems are suitable for growing on wires, on vertical posts in borders or in containers. Thornless varieties are now becoming available and are ideal in containers when there are young children running around.

Raspberries take up much less space than other cane fruits and can be grown up single posts in the border or even in containers.

Graham's top tips for raspberries

- CHOOSING VARIETIES Select for flavour, yield and season. Good choices are, in cropping order, 'Glen Moy' (thornless, midsummer); 'Glen Ample' (thornless), 'Tumaleen' (almost thornless), 'Glen Rosa' (thornless) and 'Octavia' (late summer). Good autumn varieties are 'Joan J', 'Autumn Bliss' and 'Allgold' (its yellow berries stand out well among the foliage).
- BUYING PLANTS Raspberries are rarely sold in pots, but in bundles of 6, 10 or 12 short canes. In most cases these will not fruit until their second full season, although a few varieties are now sold as 'long-cane' varieties, which fruit in their first full season and give you a quick start.
- PLANTING Raspberries are happier in partial shade than many fruits and can also be grown in containers, which should be wide and relatively shallow (like half-barrels). Plant bareroot raspberries between late autumn and late winter.

- BUYING PLANTS Blueberries are relatively slow growing so, if possible, start with large plants.
- PLANTING Are best in containers because they demand a very acid soil (very low lime) and this is much easier to provide by using ericaceous potting compost in a tub than by trying to change garden soil. Grow in partial shade.
- TRAINING AND PRUNING Remove any feeble or dead shoots.
- CARE Feed regularly but be sure to use a plant food intended for acid-loving plants.
- GOOD COMPANIONS In containers, blueberries look good alone or with hardy cyclamen around the base. In a large tub, scarlet flame flower, which is like a red perennial version of the canary creeper, is worth trying.

- TRAINING AND PRUNING When planting, cut back all except long-cane types hard. This is repeated at the end of each season for autumn-fruiting types. On summer-fruiting varieties, cut out the canes that have carried fruit immediately after cropping ceases.
- CARE Mulch every winter. Replace plants after about five years to deter viral infection. Plant new stock on a fresh site.
- GOOD COMPANIONS The necessity for summer pruning means that autumn-sown, old-fashioned sweet peas are good climbers to grow with raspberries, as are tough woodland perennials like hellebores, or with the more vigorous hardy geraniums as flowering partners at the base. Some hardy geraniums, like 'Anne Thomson', will clamber up the canes.

Strawberries

Pretty, upward-facing, white flowers and those oh-so-tempting berries are reasons enough to grow strawberries in the all-in-one garden, yet they also produce decorative, glossy, groundcovering leaves. The small-fruited, super-sweet 'alpine' strawberries are especially useful. Today's large, juicy and tasty strawberries have been developed from the wildflowers of dappled woodland, and this indicates their value in partial shade. Full shade, however, dramatically reduces the crop. Because of their questing runners, strawberries make excellent ground cover.

Strawberries not only make good ground cover in partial shade but, of course, also provide plenty of attractive and tasty fruits.

Unfortunately, strawberry plants are prone to viral diseases, so never plant runners given by friends or neighbours or those bought from plant sales and markets, because the risk of infection is high.

Graham's top tips for strawberries

- CHOOSING VARIETIES Most varieties have a specific season, but also look for flavour, yield and disease resistance. Long-season varieties like 'Alice', 'Flamenco' and 'Calypso' are especially useful, while 'Alexandria' (with green leaves), 'Golden Alexandria' (my favourite because of its dainty sweet fruits and golden yellow foliage) and 'Pegasus' have fewer runners so are more manageable in pots.

- BUYING PLANTS Runners lifted from the nursery establish well, as do plants in pots. Check on labels and in catalogues that plants are certified virus-free.
- PLANTING Plant evenly spaced in sun or damp dappled shade where small-fruited 'alpine' types are especially happy. Strawberries thrive in pots, if watered and fed well; in traditional strawberry pots they need especially careful attention to watering and feeding.
- CARE Nip back runners to ensure a full cover, but avoid crowding. Lay hay or straw mulch under the developing fruit to keep it off the muddy soil, to protect it against slugs and also to show it off well. Work mulch in among the crowns in autumn. Replace every three years, as plants inevitably become infected with virus and productivity declines. Grow new plants in a fresh site.
- GOOD COMPANIONS In a partially shaded border, treat strawberries as robust shade perennials. Grow with naturalized snowdrops and aconites, or tough perennials like hellebores, hardy geraniums, hostas and pulmonarias.

Fruit round-up

Other fruits that the all-in-one gardener might consider growing on a wall include **kiwi fruits**. These vigorous, deciduous, climbing plants feature bold, attractive foliage. They need wires on the wall for

Kiwi fruits make attractive and vigorous climbers for walls. Look out for the variety 'Jenny', the best for the all-in-one garden.

support. As they are hardy, kiwi can also be grown on a sturdy 2m (6ft) high trellis, on which they make a great background to the all-in-one border. Look for self-fertile 'Jenny'. **Passion fruit** needs a sunny wall if the most widely planted type, *Passiflora caerulea*, is to produce its orange fruits. Unfortunately these are more attractive than tasty; most types that are good for fruit need a conservatory.

Quince is more of a wall shrub than a climber and should be trained in a fan. White spring flowers are a decorative feature, followed by large, aromatic fruits and yellow autumn leaves. Choose a named variety – 'Vranja' or 'Sobu' – to be sure of good fruits.

Other large trees are also good candidates for the all-in-one garden. Many feel that **mulberries** are the most delicious and most elegant of all fruits, but they do take some years before they produce a good crop. **Nuts** are also worth considering. Walnuts and sweet chestnuts make attractive but large trees. Cobnuts have the advantage of producing flat sprays of twigs, which are ideal for staking perennials, but all nuts may be eaten by squirrels. Outstanding among nuts is the red filbert, with its red catkins and purple foliage. This superb specimen shrub is ideal behind a border.

Currants are invaluable for their fruit, but their ornamental appeal is limited unless they are grown as standards or raised in tall planters, perhaps in stained timber, so that their strings of bead-like fruits (especially of redcurrants) are well displayed. They can also be trained flat as a fan to show off the fruits. The red-fruited varieties of **gooseberries**, especially the almost thornless 'Pax', can be grown in a similar way. All make good wall or fence shrubs, where their winter structure adds an extra season of interest.

Elderberries make the most wonderful syrup or wine, and the flowers an aromatic 'champagne' or cordial. There are many varieties with eye-catching foliage – purple, variegated or prettily dissected – and these are invaluable as tough and easy-to-grow garden shrubs even if you never pick their flowers or fruit.

Finally, **citrus** are becoming ever more popular trees, especially oranges and lemons grown in containers. These thrive on the patio in summer but appreciate the protection of a conservatory, or at least a sheltered porch, in winter.

Gooseberries trained as standards add character to borders and it is easier to reach the berries to pick them.

Vegetables

For the all-in-one gardener vegetables are some of the most valuable of all plants: they have colour and flavour; they have stature and presence; they are nutritious; and seed and plants are mainly easy to find and simple to grow. They range from small and neat plants to tall and climbing ones. There are foliage variants as well as types with pretty flowers and fruits or pods. A suitable vegetable exists for every type of all-in-one garden – be it in shade or shine, wet or dry.

increasingly plants can readily be found in an ever-widening range. Some, like traditional lettuces, develop tight hearts, which are harvested whole; others produce more open growth, and individual leaves can be picked as you need them over a long period; many more can be grown as an attractive cut-and-come-again crop in a tapestry of colours in a space the size of a window-box. Most salad leaf crops are adaptable – and look great.

Salad leaves

This most adaptable group of vegetables for the all-in-one garden features wonderful colours, shapes and textures. They are easy to cultivate, and seed and

Cut-and-come-again crops

Cut-and-come-again (CCA) crops are salad leaves and leafy vegetables sown relatively thickly in a carpet or in closely spaced rows. All the fresh young

This network of different lettuce varieties creates a striking tapestry simply by being planted in a creative way.

nutritious leaves are harvested when they are 5–10cm (2–4in) high, using kitchen scissors. The plants resprout and can be cut again and usually a third time.

Although you can sow just one CCA variety, it is better for the all-in-one garden if you choose one of the mixtures. These are usually very decorative as they include a range of leaf colours and shapes. In a block in a raised bed or in a trough on the patio, balcony or deck, the prettiest pictures – both in the garden and in the salad bowl – are created from seed mixtures containing a range of different salad or stir-fry plants.

Graham's top tips for CCA

- CHOOSING VARIETIES Mixtures are sold under names like Mixed Lettuce Leaves, Mixed Salad Leaves, Saladini, Saladisi™, Mesclun Mix and so on. But try individual crops too, especially red-leaved lettuces, chicories, kales, chards and annual herbs.
- SOWING Grow in sun or, especially in late spring, in partial shade. Sow in narrow lines, broad lines, patches or carpets, according to the effect you need (see also page 25).
- CARE Make sure the soil does not dry out.
- HARVESTING Snip the leaves off just above the soil when they are 5–10cm (2–4in) high.
- GOOD COMPANIONS Are ideal around individual plants of longer term crops like red cabbages, as carpets in window-boxes and troughs, and to make short-term zigzag or curved patterns.

The finely cut foliage of endive can be left to mature into attractive rosettes, or it can be cut as a CCA salad crop.

Endive

The most attractive endive is the curled type, with its lovely rosettes of prettily dissected leaves in rather flat open heads. Leaves are picked as needed or whole heads can be cut; they can even be used as table decorations. Endive is an essential component of mixed leaf salads and is also good in CCA window-boxes and troughs.

Graham's top tips for endive

- CHOOSING VARIETIES If the selection is limited, try what's available and follow the instructions for that variety. Broad-leaved (Batavian) types are less decorative than curly types.

- **SOWING AND PLANTING** From early spring until late summer sow two seeds in each plug cell and thin to one if necessary. When growing well, plant out about 30cm (1ft) apart in good soil, which does not dry out. Summer crops will be happy in a little shade. Give early and late sowings a little protection if possible.
- **CARE** Make sure there is just one seedling at each site; water if necessary. Blanching was once routine, to reduce bitterness; modern varieties have no need.
- **HARVESTING** Cut off whole heads for salads, the stump will then resprout (sometimes twice). If then left to build up strength, spikes of blue edible flowers appear the following year. Alternatively, pick a few individual leaves from each plant over a long period.
- **GOOD COMPANIONS** The striking rounded shape of many endive plants is suitable for formal layouts with impatiens or alyssum.

Lettuce

This most valuable of the salad leaves in the all-in-one garden is available in a wide range of styles. Some develop tight hearts, while others produce a succession of loose leaves. Many have attractive reddish colouring or tints. All are decorative, but those with distinctive leaves and colouring are the most useful as they associate well with both annual and perennial flowers. Modern varieties last for longer without

This neat, double row of curly red lettuce has been interplanted with parsley and a few self-seeding violas.

running to seed, and some looseleaf varieties can be picked repeatedly for months. Lettuce is also good for CCA window-boxes and troughs, where its range of colours and textures looks delightful both while growing and in the salad bowl. Lettuce varieties are available for picking during most of the year. When they finally run to seed, dark-leaved types in particular make impressive 60cm (2ft) towers of colour.

Graham's top tips for lettuce

- **CHOOSING VARIETIES** In general, looseleaf types are good visually over a long period, whether they be oak-leaved Salad Bowl types or the more finely dissected and curly Lollo types. Some are deep red, some brighter, some merely tinted red, while others are a bright fresh green. All are good. 'Lollo Rossa', with its open hearts of crisply curled red leaves for picking over a long season, is widely available, as is 'Red Salad Bowl', with its deep red rosettes of oak-leaf shaped leaves for months.

- BUYING, SOWING AND PLANTING A limited range of plants may be on sale in garden centres, and even fewer by mail order, so if the type you want is not to be found as plants raise your own from seed – they are very easy. Sow from early spring to late summer in plug trays and thin to one seedling per cell. Then plant 23–30cm (9–12in) apart in sun in good soil which does not dry out. Lettuce can also be grown as an CCA crop (*see* page 116).
- CARE Water in dry spells. Summer crops will be happy in a little shade.
- HARVESTING Cut complete heads of hearted types, which may resprout only if cut in late winter or early spring. Looseleaf types can be picked over regularly, and this has the enormous advantage of allowing the plants to continue to contribute to the garden display. Eventually allow lettuce to run to seed and pick leaves from the extending stems.
- GOOD COMPANIONS Neater types are good in formal plantings, perhaps interplanted with impatiens, alyssum or lobelia. Are good around chives, coreopsis and other upright perennials, among nemophilas at the base of cane fruit and in a wide range of other situations.

The maturing rosettes of radicchio develop a range of leaf colours, some varieties simply flecked with red and some an altogether richer colour.

Radicchio

Radicchio, or red chicory, is a relation of endive. It makes flat red or pink rosettes followed in hearty types by tight, cabbage-like heads, which become redder as the weather cools. Non-hearty types have heads of loose leaves. Rosettes and heads can be prettily patterned with paler shades of red and with green, and both are tasty and decorative in salads. When plants are left overwinter, tall, impressive spikes of attractive edible blue flowers will appear in their second season.

Graham's top tips for radicchio

- CHOOSING VARIETIES Relatively few varieties are readily available, so try what you can get.
- SOWING AND PLANTING Plants are rarely sold. Sow two seeds in each plug cell and thin to one if necessary. When growing well, plant out about 30cm (1ft) apart in good soil, which does not dry

out. Sow from late spring to late summer for cropping from late summer into autumn. The best colour develops as the weather cools.

- CARE Remove deteriorating outer leaves.
- HARVESTING Either cut hearty types whole or remove leaves as needed; pick non-hearty types as needed. Once cut, an invaluable second crop of leaves appears.
- GOOD COMPANIONS Used in the spring bedding at Kew Gardens with blue scillas; is pretty with blue or white lobelia in summer. Radicchio is spectacular with yellow-leaved creeping Jenny (*Lysimachia nummularia* 'Aurea') underneath.

Leaf vegetables

These include many of the top-performing, all-in-one plants. They have bold structure, wonderful colours and textures, and important culinary and nutritional roles. Most leaf vegetables make a long colour contribution to the garden. They associate well with a range of flowering plants and are also good in containers. Most are easy to grow, too.

Here again, sowing seed directly into their final position in the garden is less successful aesthetically than raising seedlings in pots or plug trays and planting them out when they have reached a size at which they can make an impact. They can be raised in pots or plugs in a light but sheltered corner of the garden or sown in a seed bed and then transplanted – a greenhouse is not required.

Brussels sprouts

Purple Brussels sprouts are among the most dramatic of all-in-one vegetables. They develop an increasingly imposing presence during the summer, with their large, rounded leaves on tall plants. Then, as autumn merges into winter, the stout stems with their tightly packed buttons create a strongly vertical accent among the other garden plants.

The more familiar green varieties may be appreciated by dedicated all-in-one gardeners, but their friends and neighbours may not always share their enthusiasm. The purple-leaved sorts, often with a bluish tinge, are supreme.

Graham's top tips for sprouts

- CHOOSING VARIETIES The purple-leaved, old variety 'Rubine' has largely been supplanted by the more recent 'Falstaff', which crops better and holds its buttons for longer. These both turn green when cooked, even if steamed. The even more recent 'Red Delicious' (purple foliage and pinkish-red veins) and 'Red Bull' retain their colouring when cooked.
- SOWING AND PLANTING Sow in pots at any time from late winter until late spring. Then grow on seedlings in their own 7.5cm (3in) or 9cm (3½in) pot. Alternatively, sow a short row thinly in a seed bed, thin to 7.5cm (3in), then transplant individual plants, 60–90cm (2–3ft) apart, into good fertile soil in full sun or at least in an

Purple Brussels sprouts are spectacular in both their bold presence and in their rich colouring – and their flavour is excellent too.

buttons from each plant as they are ready. Alternatively, if the space is needed, dig up the whole plant, strip the leaves and store the stick of buttons in a cool place until it is wanted.

- GOOD COMPANIONS Blue, magenta, yellow, orange and white flowers, including those on delphiniums, cosmos and rudbeckias, are especially good companions. Canary creeper can be guided through the foliage as can sky blue morning glory, while at the back of the border clematis such as purple 'Jackmanii', pale blue 'Perle d'Azur' or white 'John Huxtable' can be guided forward from their supports. Cannas and big dahlias are also good neighbours along with the tall white *Nicotiana sylvestris*. To enhance the impact, plant in front of grey- or yellow-variegated shrubs. Finally, try guiding the stems of the vigorous hardy geranium 'Ann Folkard', with its yellowish-green leaves and magenta flowers, among the purple leaves.

open site. Do not add manure or dig the site immediately before planting.

- CARE Support plants as they develop, siting each stake so that it is hidden by the plant itself. Pull off old leaves towards the base as they deteriorate. Protect from caterpillars and from pigeons, though the latter are less troublesome in the all-in-one garden.
- HARVESTING From autumn onwards, pick a few

Cabbage

While many cabbages make relatively little impact in a garden, others create a bold impression through their colour and texture, and they do so over a long period. These are summer red cabbages, with striking and often bluish-red colouring, and winter Savoy cabbages, with attractively puckered and crinkled blue leaves. They are easy to raise, integrate well with annuals and perennials that also have a strong presence, and are less dominant than purple Brussels sprouts, although when a cabbage is finally cut for the table it does leave rather a gap in the planting scheme. The outer leaves of cabbages are an especially good source of vitamin C.

Graham's top tips for cabbages

- CHOOSING VARIETIES Mail order catalogues often provide tables of seed sowing and harvesting times for different types. Traditional varieties like 'Red Drumhead' tend to make an impact fairly quickly through their spreading early leaves, but when ready they hold their shape for less long than newer introductions. Among modern types try 'Redsky', which has good flavour and stores well, and 'Red Rookie', which can be ready in late summer.

- BUYING, SOWING AND PLANTING Young plants are sometimes available by post; pot them on for a few weeks while they become established and develop a good size before planting out. Sow red cabbage in spring and Savoy cabbages in late spring. Varieties vary in their size but planting 45cm (18in) apart in limey soil in full sun is a good guide.

- CARE Protect from caterpillars and pigeons. Remove old leaves as they become unsightly. Plants tolerate encroachment by neighbours.

- HARVESTING Red cabbage makes a feature until late autumn, when the heads can be pulled and

Cabbages bring their bold shape to plantings for a very long season, as it takes a number of months for them to mature.

stored. Savoy cabbages mature over the same period, although some varieties will last until late winter. Pull, rather than cut, cabbages so the stumps do not attract pests and diseases.

- GOOD COMPANIONS Consider a wide variety of flowers in contrasting colours or perennials with harmonizing foliage tones. Among annuals, pearly lilac petunias can carpet below and pink cosmos lean over from behind; annual rudbeckias like 'Toto' make a bolder contrast. Among perennials, clouds of white or pink gypsophila will contrast well or try coreopsis, while variegated periwinkles, blue geraniums and the delightful, yellow-eyed, blue *Viola* 'Ardross Gem' can nestle happily in front. Cabbages are lovely with chrysanthemums.

Chards

Also known as Swiss chard, seakale beet, leaf beet and spinach beet (and individual types as ruby chard or silver beet), these rather upright, very leafy plants have broad, ruffled, usually dark green foliage rising from the root. Their wide midribs and main veins are coloured in an impressive range of shades. This is another vegetable in which there has been welcome addition of new varieties recently, adding new colours to the long-lasting and manageable foliage, which eventually sprouts wild and wonderfully unruly flowering stems. In rich soil chards can be enormous, impressive yet informal, and they are best at the front of the border, often with low flowering groundcover. The fleshy midribs are often cooked separately from the green leafy blade, because their flavour is different and they take a little longer to soften. Chards also look wonderful and taste great as a CCA crop.

The red leaf stems of ruby chard make a good display even when leaves are picked for the kitchen. They also associate well with many annual flowers.

Graham's top tips for chards

- CHOOSING VARIETIES There is now a wonderful range of chard colours, all of which are found in 'Bright Lights', a mix of forms with midribs and veins in gold, pink, orange, purple, red and white, with deep and pastel variations of most shades and with green or bronzed leaves. There are individual colours, too: 'Charlotte' is scarlet, 'Silverado' has white leaf stems and midribs, 'Bright Yellow' is exactly that, 'Fantasia' is orange and 'Pink Passion' is hot purplish-pink.
- SOWING AND PLANTING Sow in spring to dazzle until autumn. Grow in plug trays or pots, then plant out 23–30cm (9–12in) apart in fertile soil, which does not dry out, in a sunny place. Sow in late summer, or early autumn, for the following spring harvest.
- CARE Chards are one of the more forgiving of vegetables, with few problems. Plants thrive

especially well when not allowed to dry out, though even in dryish conditions they often do unexpectedly well.

- HARVESTING Pick regularly and plants will keep producing more foliage. Even emerging flower stalks can be picked and steamed.
- GOOD COMPANIONS Choose prostrate verbena in appropriate colours to carpet under the chard – red verbena with white-stemmed chard, for example – or plant carpeting perennials like yellow-leaved creeping Jenny (*Lysimachia nummularia* 'Aurea'). Overwintered 'Fantasia' chard looks wonderful with daffodils.

Kale

Three types of kale are of interest to the all-in-one gardener: curly, Tuscan and ornamental kale (*see* right). Curly kale has finely crimped leaves like curly parsley in bright green or in stunning purplish red, while Tuscan kale has long slender leaves in deep blue-grey. These two are supreme in combining ornamental appeal with flavour and productivity over a long long season. In fact, curly kale and Tuscan kale are so adaptable that you can grow them either for summer or winter. Both make substantial plants, and can be placed to look great as a centrepiece in containers or as long-season foliage plants in the border. They can also be cultivated as short-season seedling crops.

Graham's top tips for kale

- CHOOSING VARIETIES Kales are not usually found in garden centres, but seed can be bought from mail order catalogues. The one variety of Tuscan kale usually seen is 'Nero di Toscano'; in curly kales look for reddish purple 'Redbor' and deep green 'Starbor' and 'Winterbor'.
- SOWING AND PLANTING Sow from mid-spring to midsummer. Move seedlings into 7.5cm (3in) or 9cm (3½in) pots to grow on before planting out from late spring to late summer in any good soil in a sunny site. Curly and Tuscan kales can also be grown as CCA crops.
- CARE Pick off any old yellowing leaves.

'Redbor' kale makes a splendid specimen plant and looks especially attractive when set in a galvanised steel container so that its foliage overhangs the edge.

The colour in ornamental kales develops best as temperatures fall during the autumn, but remember that the young leaves are tastiest.

- HARVESTING Pick individual leaves as plants mature or cut seedlings with kitchen scissors.
- GOOD COMPANIONS Red curly kale looks great with pink or purple petunias, in front of yellow-leaved shrubs, and with yellow-leaved and blue-flowered *Geranium* 'Blue Sunrise'. Try green curly kale with white annuals such as petunias, *Salvia farinacea* and bedding geraniums. Tuscan kale looks best with blue and white flowers, such as verbenas, nemesia or ageratum; alternatively, grow with perennials like border phlox and hardy geraniums, or amber or purple heucheras.

Ornamental kale

Sometimes called flowering cabbage or flowering kale, these often rather startling plants have been developed specifically as ornamentals, although some would say that garish, rather than ornamental, is the correct adjective. Ornamental kale makes a flat rosette of green, blue-green, pink and white leaves in sometimes all-too-bright combinations. It is brighter in the garden but less value in the kitchen than other kales, because only the new young central leaves are tender enough to be edible, in salads. Cooling weather in autumn encourages their best colour to develop.

Graham's top tips for flowering kale

- CHOOSING VARIETIES In garden centres buy what happens to be available. In seed catalogues you may find a choice between those with rounded leaves and those with more jagged, dissected ones. One extraordinary type is like a 'cut flower' on 60cm (2ft) stems!
- BUYING, SOWING AND PLANTING Can often be bought in small pots at garden centres and planted straight into beds or containers. Otherwise, sow in pots in early summer; move to individual pots and plant out in summer for late summer and autumn colour.
- CARE Nip off the old leaves as they deteriorate.
- HARVESTING Pick young leaves from the centre of the rosette.
- GOOD COMPANIONS Grow with dwarf asters and chrysanthemums in borders and in containers; and at the base of ornamental grasses.

Oriental vegetables

For some years the range of oriental vegetables available to gardeners has been increasing. Among those especially worth the attention of the all-in-one gardener are **purple-leaved mustards** like 'Red Giant', which are sown in summer for late autumn and winter colour and cropping. They go well with winter violas, in containers as well as beds and borders.

Pak choi, especially the white-stemmed 'Joy Choi', makes small, rapidly maturing plants that are ideal to fill gaps. When sown in summer it can be ready for cropping in six weeks. If the heads are cut off, rather than plants pulled, they will resprout.

Mizuna has sharply toothed leaves a little like endive's and is more resistant to bolting than many oriental vegetables grown in the West. It has a long season: when cut in summer it regrows – two or three times – and it looks good through winter. Eventually it bears pretty yellow flowers. Sow over snowdrops for spring; it also makes good short-term edging. It is often included in Mesclun CCA mixes.

Rhubarb

This classic 'is-it-a-vegetable-or-a-fruit' crop is actually a culinary hardy perennial. Its dramatic, red-stemmed foliage is a feature, and although the towering, late-season, creamy plumes are often removed, they do in fact make an important contribution to the all-in-one garden. Rhubarb tolerates poor conditions but repays richer fare and will tolerate some shade.

Forcing rhubarb creates the tastiest stalks and if you choose an elegant forcing pot this will add extra interest to the garden all the year round.

Graham's top tips for rhubarb

- CHOOSING VARIETIES All named varieties should be good, while unnamed plants from a neighbour or local market will usually be much less reliable. 'Stockbridge Arrow' is an excellent variety'; 'Timperley Early' will mature a week or so earlier.

- BUYING AND PLANTING Rhubarb is sold in pots or as crowns dug from the ground. Crowns are often larger than pot-grown plants yet may establish less quickly. Plant in any good soil in full sun or a little shade. Rhubarb is ideal as a bold back-of-the-border plant.
- CARE Leave to establish without cropping in the first year. Mulch well in autumn after cutting back to the crown. Blanch stems with an elegant rhubarb forcing pot or a large bin.
- GOOD COMPANIONS Plant with late-flowering, contrasting perennials like asters, actaeas and hardy chrysanthemums with a hedge or dark shrub behind to set off the flowers.

Seakale

This wonderful perennial, which can be found growing wild on gravelly beaches across Europe, is rather different from many all-in-one vegetables as it appreciates dry, well-drained conditions and can withstand salt spray. It is attractive right from the moment its purple shoots emerge through the gravel in which it is best grown. Wavy, bluish, rather cabbage-like foliage is followed by clouds of white flowers. Even without its edible qualities, seakale deserves a place in a Mediterranean or gravel garden, growing among bushy herbs and bulbs. Blanch the young shoots by covering the plant with a seakale pot. This closed decorative terracotta pot can itself make an eye-catching garden feature while it does its work.

Pod plants

Two invaluable vegetable groups fit in here: beans and peas. Beans are grown not only for their flowers, some of which are pretty enough to grow even if there were no pods, but also for their coloured pods. They come in climbing and bush forms, and the purple-podded types are reckoned to have the best flavour but do turn green when cooked. The lablab bean is perhaps the most attractive of all beans, but is not eaten very widely. Peas are less effective in flower and there is less choice for pods, although there is unexpected value in the leafless types.

All pod plants have the advantage of having large, easy-to-handle seeds. Relatively few varieties that are of interest to the all-in-one gardener are on sale as plants, and their availability is unpredictable. Leave the roots of all peas and beans in place at the end of the season because they return useful plant foods to the soil.

Broad beans

Broad beans are hardy and bold, and have stout upright stems lined with flowers held in the leaf joints. Most bear attractive white or purplish flowers with a dark chocolate stamp at the centre, but they can be a little murky in colour, never quite white. Broad bean flowers have a noticeably sweet scent, though it does not carry well. There is also a superb red-flowered variety. The pods are fat and green, being striking rather than especially decorative. Dwarf varieties crowd their flowers and leaves on to short stems; taller types have real impact but need staking.

Graham's top tips for broad beans

- CHOOSING VARIETIES 'Crimson Flowered' has wonderful rich crimson flowers with white tubes lining the vertical stems followed by relatively short pods. It is hard to find but worth searching out. Otherwise look for: 'Dreadnought' and 'Imperial Green Longpod', for long-podded, tall plants; 'The Sutton' and 'Optica' for short plants; and 'The Sutton' or 'Aquadulce Claudia' for autumn sowing.
- SOWING AND PLANTING Sow pairs of seeds in 7.5cm (3in) pots from early spring, then thin to one. Plant out 23–30cm (9–12in) apart in a sunny site. Some varieties can also be sown in autumn for spring flowering and cropping.
- CARE Deal with black fly promptly. Tall types may need discreet support.

Crimson-flowered broad beans are well worth growing for their flowers alone but, as with other broad bean varieties, the flowers are followed by pods of tasty beans.

Climbing runner beans feature broad foliage, red, pink, white or bicoloured flowers and long pods of tasty beans.

- HARVESTING Keep picking regularly to ensure a long season of flowers.
- GOOD COMPANIONS 'Crimson Flowered' and dwarf types are wonderful in containers, where you can smell them. Clouds of trailing lobelia and bacopa make good partners. Autumn-sown, tall types look good among perennials like asters and chrysanthemums, which will fill in their space when they are removed.

Climbing beans

These fall into two categories: runner beans, with flat pods; and climbing French beans, generally with round pods. They are both worth growing for their flowers, too. A few climbing French beans are cultivated for flowers and pods; they also have the additional advantage of producing pods without pollination by bees, unlike runners, whose cropping can therefore be more unpredictable. There is also one invaluable foliage variety of runner bean.

Graham's top tips for climbing beans

- CHOOSING VARIETIES For flowers use runner beans like 'Painted Lady' (red and white bicolour), 'Sunset' (apricot pink), 'Celebration' (pale salmon), 'Riley' (rose pink) or 'White Lady' (white); most of the rest bear brilliant scarlet flowers. 'Sunbright' has a bright combination of goldish-green leaves and scarlet flowers and is also less vigorous and so

lighter in weight. 'Purple Podded' is a self-explanatory, climbing, pencil-podded French bean with sultry purple flowers. Look too for purple-podded 'Trionfo' and stringless 'Blauhilde' and 'Empress'. 'Borlotto Lingua di Fuoco' ('Firetongue') has white pods boldly splashed in red (they make good table decorations) and similarly speckled seeds.

- BUYING, SOWING AND PLANTING Runner bean plants are sometimes available in garden centres. Or sow two seeds in a 7.5cm (3in) pot in spring, then thin to one; plant out after the last frosts in a sunny site. Dig the soil thoroughly and deeply so plants can absorb the nutrients and moisture. Be sure to allow access for picking. Support plants either on a stout vertical cylinder of wire mesh; a line of wire or heavy duty plastic mesh; mesh fixed to a fence; or traditional wigwams of canes or rustic poles. Climbing beans produce a great deal of growth and so-called pea and bean netting may collapse; they are also too heavy to train through all but the stoutest shrubs.

- CARE Watering is crucial in keeping the flowers coming and, in runners, ensuring a good set of pods; it is done most effectively in the evening. Drip or trickle irrigation is the wisest approach, but a regular bucketful will do.
- HARVESTING There is a balance to be struck between enjoying the coloured pods and picking them to encourage more, because flowering and cropping will tail off if the pods are left on the plants. With runners grown for their flowers it is clear where the balance lies.
- GOOD COMPANIONS Are usually best as a background for other plants or as a vertical accent through which climbing annual convolvulus can twine.

Dwarf beans

Dwarf beans make bushy plants up to 60cm (2ft) high with compact growth. Again, there are two distinct types that have slightly different attractions: dwarf runners are cultivated for their flowers, while dwarf French beans are grown for purple flowers and pods or their golden pods. In some cases the flowers may be hidden by foliage, yet some dwarf runners hold their flowers outside the leaves, and some dwarf French beans now carry their flowers and pods above the leaves.

Graham's top tips for dwarf beans

- CHOOSING VARIETIES In dwarf runners go for 'Gulliver' or 'Pickwick' (both red flowers), 'Snow White' (white flowers) and best of all 'Hestia' (red-and-white, bicoloured flowers); a mix of all three is sometimes seen. 'Purple Tepee' is a dwarf French bean that holds its purple pods (and purple flowers) above the leaves; 'Purpuriat' does not, but keeps its purple colour after steaming. 'Golden Tepee' has bright yellow pods above the leaves.
- SOWING AND PLANTING Plants are rarely available, so sow seeds in pairs in 7.5cm (3in) pots in spring, then thin to one; plant out after the last frosts in a sunny site. Prepare the soil well, to

Dwarf bean varieties that hold their beans above the foliage are especially useful as they show up well and are also easy to pick.

provide continuing moisture and nutrients. Dwarf runners also make good container plants and are more practical than climbing runners in many situations.

- CARE Consistent moisture helps continuing flowering and cropping in all dwarf beans, but make sure that runners do not dry out or the flowers may not set to pods.
- HARVESTING Pick regularly, or dead-head, to keep the flowers coming.
- GOOD COMPANIONS Among annuals trailing blue lobelia, blue torenia, trailing antirrhinums, white bacopa and mini petunias all make good partners. In perennials try yellow-leaved creeping Jenny (*Lysimachia nummularia* 'Aurea') running underneath, and alongside plant low hardy geraniums, dwarf golden rod and dwarf kniphofias.

Lablab beans

Also known as the hyacinth bean and hyacinth runner bean, this is probably the most attractive of the beans but the least often grown and the least appreciated in the kitchen, where stir-frying its flat pods is the best approach. In the variant usually seen, the scented, purplish or pink-and-white, two-tone flowers give way to shining magenta pods all carried on wine-tinted, dark green foliage. Lablab beans are best in high temperatures and languish if the summer is too cool.

Graham's top tips for lablab beans

- CHOOSING VARIETIES 'Ruby Moon' has dark foliage and is disease resistant.
- SOWING AND PLANTING Sow seeds individually in 7.5cm (3in) or 9cm (3½in) pots at 21°C (70°F). Once there is less risk of frost, plant in rich soil by a sunny, sheltered wall. Support with strong netting, trellis or a stout shrub. In hot areas and hot summers stems may reach 5m (15ft).
- CARE Keep well watered.
- HARVESTING Pick the flat pods while they are still flat. The flowers are edible, too.
- GOOD COMPANIONS White morning glory is ideal or deep blue 'Star of Yelta'.

Peas

Peas climb using tendrils at the ends of their leaves and develop white or purplish flowers in the leaf joints followed by pods in twos and threes. The flowers are pretty enough but hardly outstanding, so the all-in-one gardener should plant the hard-to-find, purple-podded variety. So-called leafless peas, where many of the leaves are transformed into a mass of interlocking (and edible) tendrils, are also useful, especially in supporting tall, top-heavy bulbs.

Graham's top tips for peas

- CHOOSING VARIETIES 'Purple Podded' may be only available from specialists. Good 'leafless' peas include 'Canoe' and 'Markana'.

Purple podded peas bring unexpected colour to the pea crop and when picked at this early mange tout stage are especially tender and tasty.

- SOWING AND PLANTING From early spring to midsummer sow seeds in pairs in 7.5cm (3in) pots, then plant 15cm (6in) apart in rich, well-prepared soil in a sunny place. Well-spaced plants crop for longer than crowded ones.
- CARE Keep well watered. Protect seeds against mice. Support with towers of wire mesh or 'baskets' of secure brushwood. 'Leafless' peas need little more than a few brushwood twigs.
- HARVESTING Keep picking regularly. Eat 'Purple Podded' when small, even as a mangetout, and harvest 'leafless' peas before they become large and starchy.
- GOOD COMPANIONS Plant 'Purple Podded' towards the front of a border, where its pretty purple flowers can be seen alongside sweet peas such as 'Cupani's Original', in which the flower size is not out of proportion. Plant tall alliums to grow through 'leafless' peas.

The tomato family

Aubergines, peppers and tomatoes are all frost-tender relations of the potato, and they thrive in sunny beds and borders and in containers. They are available in an increasing variety of plant sizes, colours, growth habits and fruit shapes for an increasing range of situations, so are good value in the all-in-one garden.

Aubergines (eggplants)

Aubergines demand the warmest conditions. Their lilac-purple flowers are attractive but usually hidden under their large, paddle-shaped leaves, as are their fruits. These can be few and huge, or small and more prolific – and not necessarily purple. In general the smaller fruited, white or white-striped varieties of aubergines are more showy.

Graham's top tips for aubergines

- CHOOSING VARIETIES Small-fruited, compact, white varieties are best for the all-in-one garden, so look for 'Mohican'. 'Fairy Tale' with its long, purple-and-white-striped fruits on compact plants is also a good choice. Asian varieties, with their long cylindrical fruits, are also worth growing.
- BUYING, SOWING AND PLANTING Plants are occasionally available. Sow seed at 16–18°C (61–64°F) in spring. Move seedlings into 9cm (3½in) pots. When all danger of frost is passed, plant out, 38–45cm (15–18in) apart, in warm,

Aubergines do well in a container on a sheltered patio and, with extra tasty French parsley planted around the base, they make an effective feature.

sheltered ground or set in tubs or other containers in an open porch or other warm, sheltered area, because aubergines revel in warm conditions. Small-fruited, white varieties can be decorative in a conservatory.

- CARE Keep well watered and fed with tomato feed. A moist atmosphere assists fruit set and growth; hot, dry conditions encourage pests. Tie back leaves discreetly to show off fruits.
- HARVESTING Pick as the fruits ripen to keep them coming.
- GOOD COMPANIONS Thunbergias enjoy the same sheltered conditions as aubergines.

Peppers

Yet again, recent developments by plant breeders are on the side of the all-in-one gardener, both for sweet (bell) peppers and for hot (and not so hot) chilli peppers. Peppers generally grow on rather upright plants with bright green stems and leaves. They are more demanding of high temperature than tomatoes, but less so than aubergines.

There are now pepper varieties created specially for containers, even semi-trailing types for hanging baskets. Some also hold their fruits away from the main stem, where they can be seen easily, and others are tolerant of cooler summers. A whole range of fruit colours has been developed, and there are even pretty varieties with masses of tiny fruits, often grown as cut 'flowers' rather than as edibles, or with purple or variegated foliage.

Graham's top tips for peppers

- CHOOSING VARIETIES In sweet (bell) peppers, 'Mohawk' (orange fruit, trailing habit), 'Redskin' (red fruits, upright), 'Sweet Orange Baby' (orange fruit, upright) are good outside in relatively cool climates (like Britain's); a far wider range will thrive in warmer climates. In chilli peppers, try 'Apache' (red fruits, bushy) and 'Cheyenne' (orange fruits, semi-trailing). 'Medusa' (yellow and red chillies on top of the plant, like spiky hair) needs warmer conditions. Dark-leaved chillies, like 'Pretty in Purple'

Tomatoes

The all-in-one gardener looks for colour in tomatoes. Thus the long scarlet, yellow or orange bead strings of cherry tomatoes are a top choice, especially as the small, yellowish-green flowers also make an impact. The increasing range of hanging basket varieties can also be used as bed edging, as can neat and sprawling bush types. Tomatoes are good in containers and in a sunny border – the warmer the better – and cherry tomatoes in particular crop over a long season.

Modern varieties of pepper are suited to growing in containers on the patio and even in hanging baskets as well as in sheltered beds and borders.

(deep purple then red fruits), can be hard to find, as are those with speckled foliage.

- BUYING, SOWING AND PLANTING Young plants, especially of outdoor container varieties of chilli peppers, are available by mail order. Sow seed at 21°C (70°F). If possible, move containers into a cool greenhouse or conservatory before planting outside. Harden off well before planting out, once there is little risk of frost; spacing depends on the variety.
- CARE Water and feed with tomato feed regularly.
- HARVESTING Pick as soon as peppers are usable – the flavour becoming hotter, and the colour often changing, as they mature.
- GOOD COMPANIONS Bushy annuals like petunias, tagetes and salvias are useful around the base of upright sorts. Or semi-trailing peppers can go round the base of upright peppers, with blue trailing lobelia in between. In sheltered corners plume-like, orange or yellow celosias are good, especially with 'Medusa'.

Graham's top tips for tomatoes

- CHOOSING VARIETIES For containers and edging try 'Tumbling Tom' (in red and in yellow), or just one plant of 'Tumbler' (red) in a hanging basket. 'Totem' (red) is dwarf, upright but not elegant. For larger containers and borders select 'Gardener's Delight' (red) and the attractively striped 'Tigerella' for flavour, 'Sweet Million' (red), 'Sungold' (orange) and 'Ildi' (yellow) for long strings. Productive bush types for borders and raised beds include 'Tornado' and 'Red Alert'.
- BUYING, SOWING AND PLANTING Plants are often available in garden centres and by post. Sow at 20°C (68°F), move into 9cm (3½in) pots; then plant outside after the last frost or into containers indoors to be moved out later. Spacing depends on the variety. Sun is essential – the more warmth there is, the

'Gardeners Delight' is a traditional tomato which is one of the best for growing outside and combines a heavy crop with a lovely flavour.

better the crop and flavour will be.

- CARE For the all-in-one gardener generous watering and feeding are essential, as although the flavour may be better developed in starved plants they look tatty and unattractive. Stake tall types or train against a sunny wall.
- HARVESTING Pick as the fruits ripen. In some cherry varieties you may be harvesting the fruits on the same cluster that flowers are still opening at the other end.
- GOOD COMPANIONS In baskets mini petunias are good, as are less overpowering flowering plants like summer violas; as edging grow with single French marigolds. Bush types in borders look good with tall, more robust French marigolds or with groundcover petunias. Taller tomatoes will support lightweight climbers; plant bushy annuals, like the larger bedding geraniums or mounding groundcover petunias, around the base to hide their bare stems.

The pumpkin family

Courgettes (zucchini), cucumbers, melons, pumpkins, squashes – bushy or much more rampageous types – all belong to the same family. They start life in much the same way, by forming big leaves and large flowers and the fruits they develop can grow to be enormous. Then they diverge, and cucumbers pass out of the attention of the all-in-one gardener; their leaves may be bold and striking but their additional attractions are few. Although the flowers of all these plants are sometimes held clear, their leaves tend to hide what can be colourful and interestingly shaped fruits; only some pumpkins are sufficiently large to obtrude, and only some courgettes are brightly coloured enough so that they glint through the foliage.

Courgette (zucchini) and marrows (summer squash)

Names can be confusing. Courgettes, in Europe, are known as zucchini in America; a marrow is a courgette intended to be grown to a much larger size and is known as summer squash in America. Most of these fruits grow on compact bushy plants with foliage that is often silvered. Climbing types can be trained either against fences or on stout wires, and have considerable appeal. Yellow-fruited types show up best against the foliage. The yellow flowers are also edible; use them deep fried or stuffed. Pick the fruits when they are very small for extra tenderness and to keep the plants cropping.

Graham's top tips for courgettes

- CHOOSING VARIETIES Courgette 'Black Forest' (deep green) is a climber for fences or trellis and can also be grown in containers. Climbing 'Trombocino' bears huge yellow flowers, then pale green fruits, which can be picked when small before they become almost circular and pale yellow – quite a spectacle. Good yellow bush types include 'Orelia' and disease-resistant 'Soleil'. Spherical 'One Ball', disease-resistant 'Defender' and the compact 'Venus' are outstanding among green varieties. For marrows (summer squashes) disease-resistant 'Tiger Cross' is a fine bush type and 'Long Green' is a good climber.
- BUYING, SOWING AND PLANTING Plants, in a limited range, are sometimes seen in garden centres and mail order catalogues. Sow seeds singly in 7.5cm (3in) or 9cm (3½in) pots at 15°C (59°F). Once there is little risk of frost in your area plant them out in sun and good soil before they become pot-bound. Spacing depends on the type (climbing or bushy) and the variety.
- CARE Water generously in dry spells. Guide trailers into open areas or cut them back.
- HARVESTING Pick courgettes regularly to keep them coming. If grown for marrows (summer squash) restrict the number allowed to develop or cropping may stop and size may also be reduced.

Yellow-fruited courgette (zucchini) varieties taste just as good, if not better than, green-fruited sorts but make so much more impact in the garden.

- GOOD COMPANIONS Bush types make excellent groundcover but need bold companions that can hold their own against such dominant foliage: try tall Spuria irises, asters, the more substantial kniphofias and sunflowers. Climbing types, on fences and trellis, look good with any sun-loving annual climbers.

Pumpkins and winter squashes

These can be spectacular, either in size or quantity, and come in an extraordinary range of colours, shapes and sizes. Growth tends to be vigorous, making these plants splendid groundcover in new gardens and spectacular on a trellis, although some large-fruited pumpkins grown against a trellis will probably respond disastrously to the call of gravity. They demand plenty of water, although the large leaves of even well-watered plants may still wilt in the sun. Many pumpkins and winter squashes look their best towards autumn, as the leaves fall away and the fruits are revealed. Some will thrive only in very warm summer climates. Many are invaluable when picked and used as decorative additions to patios and steps.

Graham's top tips for pumpkins

- CHOOSING VARIETIES For Halloween pumpkins of 2.5–3kg (5½–6½lb) try 'Mars' or 'Orbit', and for absolute monsters go for 'Atlantic Giant'. Otherwise select the type you like from your favourite seed catalogue.
- BUYING, SOWING AND PLANTING Plants, often unnamed, may be available from garden

The foliage of pumpkins is large and vigorous and when fed and watered well the plants produce plenty of fruits late in the season.

centres. It is easy to raise seed sown singly in 7.5cm (3in) or 9cm (3½in) pots at 20°C (68°F) about six to eight weeks before your last frost date. Plant out in good soil in full sun, once there is little risk of frost.
- CARE Provide robust support for climbing plants. For monster but inedible pumpkins remove all but one or two fruits when small.
- HARVESTING Pick for fresh use as needed. Leave those for storing on the plants as long as possible so their skins harden in the sun.
- GOOD COMPANIONS In the open ground choose robust plants like bold clumps of sunflowers or hollyhocks and copses of sweetcorn to stand up to a determined pumpkin. Annual climbers are the best companions on fences and trellis.

The onion family

This is a rather diverse group, except for its similarity in smell and its black angular seeds, which grow through different seasons and mature at different times. Leeks are an especially important constituent of the all-in-one garden in autumn and winter. All members of the onion family are easy to grow, and although each has its particular needs none is fussy.

Leeks

The white stems of this unexpectedly versatile vegetable erupt into a mass of bold and impressive broad foliage. They are grown to their fat maturity for winter, and they make an important cold weather feature, with their bluish-green flags silvered in frost. When planted in clusters, leeks are also useful as tasty spring onion alternatives.

Graham's top tips for leeks

- CHOOSING VARIETIES Late varieties are the hardiest, and also feature the best blue colouring. 'Apollo' has especially good blue leaves and is disease resistant, as is 'Porvite'. Early varieties like 'King Richard' and 'Titan' work well as mini leeks.
- BUYING, SOWING AND PLANTING Plug plants are offered by mail order, and these are excellent. Otherwise, sow in spring, in plug trays or small pots, and plant out singly 23cm (9in) apart when 23cm (9in) high. To multi-sow leeks, sow three or four seeds in a plug cell and plant as a group. Wider spacings give bigger but fewer leeks and allow interplanting. For long, white stems, plant deeply. Grow in rich soil in sun.
- CARE Keep weed free and allow only low creeping companions. A liquid feed is beneficial.
- HARVESTING Leave in place until needed; even mini leeks will last well. In spring impressive flower stems erupt on any leeks still *in situ*.
- GOOD COMPANIONS Interplant with lettuce when the plants are young. In winter leeks look good when lined up in a board-edged raised bed or set against curly kale.

In winter, leeks develop a noticeably bluer colouring and make bold and impressive plants, especially as their leaves hang over the clean lines of the edge of the bed.

Onions

Bulb onions are essential kitchen fare and also striking plants for the garden because of their upright, cylindrical leaves. But they dislike competition from other plants (including weeds), which leads to smaller onions, so they are not easy to grow in the all-in-one garden. Onions grow better in raised beds and potagers than in mixed borders. Red-skinned varieties are more striking than yellow- and white-skinned types and have a richer, milder flavour. Onions are grown in two ways: from seed sown in spring; and from sets, which are mini onions about the size of marbles. The latter are much simpler to grow than seed; they are less troubled by pests and diseases and get off to a quick start, so they make an impact sooner.

Graham's top tips for onions

- CHOOSING VARIETIES Red onions have the most visual impact; look for 'Red Barron' as sets or seed or seed of 'Red Pearl'. For yellow onions try sets of 'Sturon' or, for entertainingly huge onions, 'Showmaster'.
- BUYING, SOWING AND PLANTING Young plants are rarely seen for sale while sets are widely available; always buy the heat-treated type, which do not run to seed prematurely. Plant in spring in a sunny site. (Never plant late; onions do not catch up.) Also sow seed in plugs, thinned to one plant; for a heavier crop of smaller onions and a spikier look, sow three or four seeds to a plug and plant as a clump.
- CARE Water plants when young, and keep the planting site weed free.
- HARVESTING Dig up only once the tops have fallen over, in summer. Never force over onion foliage, because this encourages disease.
- GOOD COMPANIONS Grow in blocks in raised beds surrounded by clumps of contrasting but not dominant plants such as rounded looseleaf lettuce. Alternatively, interplant with lettuce at generous spacings. The tiniest annuals, like violet cress, dainty yellow saxifrage or the smallest violas can be scattered among the onion sets without harm.

Given space to grow, onions can develop to a large size; when planted more closely together, you get a heavier crop of smaller onions.

Spring onions (scallions)

These small onions provide a quick upright accent as well as invaluable saladings. Red-skinned varieties with their dark green leaves are becoming more widespread and add extra appeal. Sow thinly where they are to be cropped, in good soil in an open position, and about 2.5cm (1in) apart if possible; keep weed free. Spring onions will be ready for harvesting about three months after sowing, but they can form fat, fiercely flavoured bulbs if left longer. 'White Lisbon' is a useful old favourite and has a hardy variant for overwintering. Also look for red-skinned, dark-leaved types, like 'Redmate' and 'Furio'.

Root vegetables

Inevitably, the aesthetic appeal of a root vegetable is largely limited to its foliage, and in some – turnips and swedes, for example – this is insufficient to tempt the all-in-one gardener. In beetroot and carrots, however, the foliage has some appeal, while the flowers of potatoes are sufficiently attractive for them to have been used in the summer display in front of the Palm House at Kew.

Beetroot

All beetroot has attractive reddish veins in the dark green foliage, which makes a prompt impact, forming an upright and arching rosette above the expanding root. A few old varieties produce glossy, deep reddish-purple leaves, and these were widely used in public bedding displays many decades ago. The trade-off to be considered is that those with the best foliage have less good roots for kitchen use and vice versa. The youngest leaves are delicious in salads.

Graham's top tips for beetroot

- CHOOSING VARIETIES For the best leaf colour but unremarkable flavour try 'Bull's Blood' (broad leaves) and 'MacGregor's Favourite' (very appealing, strap-shaped leaves). 'Boltardy' has excellent flavour, and 'Modena' is a 'monogerm' (see below) with good all-round qualities. 'Burpee's Golden' has orange roots and yellow-veined, pale green leaves. 'Cook's Delight' is a

good compromise between colour and culinary excellence. Some modern varieties have relatively dull, plain green leaves.

- SOWING AND PLANTING Sow in plugs in spring and plant 10–15cm (4–6in) apart in good soil in a sunny place. (It dislikes poor soil.) Beetroot 'seeds' usually consist of a cluster of two or three seeds so a little group of seedlings may emerge. This makes a less elegant rosette, and misshapen or tangled roots, so either choose the so-called 'monogerm' varieties (with just one seed per cluster) or thin seedlings to one by cutting off the extras with scissors.
- CARE Tidy the foliage of late sowings in autumn.
- HARVESTING Small roots can be ready in 10 weeks. Beetroot can be left for a longer display and

The foliage of all beetroot plants is attractive but varieties with the best roots, grown for the kitchen, may not have the rich red colour of those grown specifically for their foliage.

The feathery foliage of carrots is very attractive at close quarters and is a valuable partner for plants that have broader and glossier leaves.

then dug up for immediate use or storage.

- GOOD COMPANIONS Is very adaptable and good in summer with French marigolds, white verbenas and red-and-white bedding geraniums. Overwinter with blue or white violas or winter pansies with blue-and-white nemophilas or yellow-and-white limnanthes for spring. Beetroot is useful as edging, and to outline plantings and make patterns.

Carrots

Carrots can be a difficult crop for the all-in-one gardener. Their eruptive plumes of fine, feathery foliage are very pretty, yet carrot roots are prone to pest attack, for which resistant varieties are only partially effective. All but the short, round varieties, which do not last well once mature, are best sown where they are to grow. This necessitates a period of low interest in the carrot plot while the plants develop. In addition to the traditional orange roots, purple-, white- and yellow-rooted carrots are available.

Graham's top tips for carrots

- CHOOSING VARIETIES 'Parmex' is a good round carrot. 'Flyaway' and 'Resistafly' are carrotfly-resistant varieties; both are long rooted.
- SOWING AND PLANTING In spring sow round varieties in plugs in twos and threes, and plant out unthinned, about 10cm (4in) apart, in sun and well-drained soil. Thin long-rooted carrots to one seedling and plant when young, before the extending taproot becomes restricted; or, better still, sow direct in the open.
- CARE Keep weed-free when young. Provide even moisture, to prevent roots splitting.
- HARVESTING Pull when ready, having watered the soil first in dry weather. If left too long in the soil, roots of some may become tough. Pick small roots for gourmet salads.
- GOOD COMPANIONS The fine foliage of carrots looks good with broad-leaved plants like beetroot or, among perennials, heucheras. Carrots are also ideal alternating or interplanted with impatiens, alyssum and lobelia.

Potatoes

The idea of growing potatoes for their flowers may seem hard to believe, but they can be attractive in the border, perhaps around bold foliage plants like phormiums. The flowers are usually lilac or white with a yellow centre, and it has to be admitted that the impact of the flowers in relation to the size of the plants is modest, because potatoes are large plants. However, 'Duke of York' bears interesting large white flowers with a slight blush, and 'Golden Wonder' has blooms in shades of lilac with white-tipped petals. Plants need support after flowering, when the tops tend to flop.

Vegetable round-up

The more space you have for vegetables, the more you can try, and the following are all well worth considering for the all-in-one garden.

Purple-sprouting broccoli makes an imposing specimen in winter, although it often loses its lower leaves, which detracts from the display, and it may need staking. Just pick the small spears as you need them. **Orache** is a leafy little vegetable and, especially in its purple-leaved variants, is decorative from its seedling stage to its maturity as a 2m (6ft) spire. The smallest leaves are the only ones worth picking for food. The perennial **red-veined dock** has bright green leaves with dramatic red veins in generous rosettes. All but the youngest leaves may need blanching to increase their tenderness.

Sweetcorn makes a bold and imposing plant for a long season and the pale streak along the centre of each leaf adds interest when seen close to.

Rocket is a quick-growing salad crop of rather spicily flavoured, fresh green leaves, which is at its most decorative as it runs up to flower. However, at this stage its leaves become rather too powerfully flavoured. Rocket flowers are edible. Unfortunately, rocket is susceptible to flea beetle, which ruins both its look and its kitchen value.

The upright stature of **sweetcorn**, with its long, pale-centred leaves, is dramatic, and there is no other vegetable quite like it. It can make a lovely architectural feature against a dark wooden shed or summerhouse. Unfortunately, those with ornamental foliage, like the pink-and-white striped 'Quadricolor', have poor cobs (or none in cooler climates). The colour in those with ornamental cobs is not apparent in the garden, so the best croppers have only their stature to recommend them. Sow individually in pots and plant out after the last frost.

Herbs

Herbs offer invaluable options to the all-in-one gardener, so much so that many of these plants are already grown as ornamentals by gardeners with little interest in any practical use for their plants or any particular interest in herbs. It is, almost without exception, their foliage that marks out herbs, and this provides a long season of ornamental, culinary and often fragrant interest.

Basil

The soft foliage of basil with its wonderful Mediterranean aroma is a tempting plant for the all-in-one gardener, especially those variants with muted purple foliage. It makes upright growth of rather soft stems. Basil has always been a borderline plant in temperate climates, and it needs warm summers and especially warm summer nights to grow well. It is often best cultivated in individual containers on a patio or balcony, where it can be sited close to a wall, which will retain overnight warmth. As with so many all-in-one plants, new varieties have provided more interesting options than just plain green plants.

Graham's top tips for basil

- CHOOSING VARIETIES Purple-leaved basil, sometimes listed simply as 'red' or 'purple' and sometimes as 'Red Rubin' or 'Arrarat', is the top choice for foliage. Also try 'Siam Queen', a slightly liquorice-flavoured variety with more striking purple flowers, or one of the other unusual-flavoured varieties. The miniature-leaved types, always green, are also highly ornamental and make a good low hedge or punctuation mark.
- BUYING, SOWING AND PLANTING Plants are sometimes available by mail order. Be wary of garden centre plants, which may have been chilled or allowed to dry out. Sow seed at 21°C (70°F) in spring, then move into individual pots. After the last frost, plant out in a rich, sunny, sheltered place or leave plants in containers.
- CARE Keep warm, well watered and fed. As with tomatoes, the less water and food basil is given

Basil is a herb that appreciates a warm situation and if grown near a wall will benefit at night from the heat stored in the brickwork during the day.

the better the flavour but growth is reduced. Pinch out flowering tips, and use as a garnish.

- HARVESTING Pick leaves and shoot tips as needed. New growth will appear from lower down.
- GOOD COMPANIONS Containers of purple basil look good among single French marigolds. Green basil looks especially fresh with white alyssum at the base.

Bay

This invaluable plant, both in the garden and kitchen, is unexpectedly tough and forms an impressive evergreen shrub or even a small tree with aromatic, leathery leaves. Bay is ideal as a garden feature, as a hedge and as a component of Mediterranean settings, and it looks good in containers. It can be trained into pyramids and balls and decorated with Christmas lights in tubs outside the front door.

Graham's top tips for bay

- CHOOSING VARIETIES Basically there are only two: the familiar, green-leaved *Laurus nobilis*, and the yellow-leaved *L. nobilis* 'Aurea', which looks fine when growing well but sickly when not.
- SOWING AND PLANTING Can be slow to start from seed so instead buy plants. Bay is always available in garden centres, which often sell specimen-sized plants. Plant in full sun in any good soil that is not waterlogged. Avoid exposure to cold winds.

Bay trees can be bought as small plants but over the years can develop into large trees unless trimmed; in pots they are especially effective and do not grow too large.

- CARE Keep container-grown plants well watered and trim them as necessary. Tidy plants in spring and reduce in size if necessary.
- HARVESTING Nipping off shoots as they are needed often helps to keep plants trim, so pruning is unnecessary. Otherwise, clip them over in late summer.
- GOOD COMPANIONS Bay is excellent for providing gravitas in a Mediterranean garden, as a standard in a potager with clipped box hedge as edging. In a container it is often grown without partners.

Chives

This indispensable perennial, with its tight clumps of slender, tubular leaves topped with round heads of usually pink or lilac, or perhaps white, flowers, is an easy, tolerant and colourful herb. Its leaves and edible flowers provide mild onion flavour for many months.

Graham's top tips for chives

- CHOOSING VARIETIES Look for the very useful dwarf varieties, which are even suitable for window-boxes; they include the white-flowered 'Corsican White', ivory 'Wallington White', rose-pink 'Polyphant' and tiny white 'Silver Chimes'. Purplish-pink 'Forescate' is taller and the most colourful and productive. There is even a rare variant with twisted leaves.
- BUYING, SOWING AND PLANTING Buy as plants (though easily raised from seed) as this allows you to choose named varieties in different flower colours and heights. Plant in sunny or slightly shaded situations in any reasonable soil. Chives are also successful as container-grown plants.
- CARE Divide plants every two or three years to help maintain good vigour. Water in long dry spells to keep leaves developing.
- HARVESTING Snip off whole leaves and flower stems, a few from each plant, so plants continue to look attractive while still providing the flavour you need.
- GOOD COMPANIONS The shortest types of chives are good edging and window-box plants when planted with broader-leaved plants like bronze and purplish-toned heucheras or hostas in yellow or bluish colour. All chives hold their own well in the rough and tumble of mixed borders.

Coriander (cilantro) is an intensely aromatic herb that can be grown in pots or in the border; in either case, keep it moist to help prevent it from running to seed.

Coriander (cilantro)

The leaves and stems of coriander are sometimes known as cilantro, to distinguish them from the seeds, which are often ground for cooking. It has a short season of aromatic foliage, as plants produce their lacy little white flowers a little early. Allow plants to self-sow through informal plantings in a little shade (which helps delay flowering) and pick leaves as and when you need them. For the most leaves choose varieties specifically intended for leaf production. These are available from herb specialists.

Dill

Dill and fennel look similar with their leaves divided into the most slender, slightly blue-green segments and usually held on just a single stem topped with flat heads of yellowish flowers. Dill's flavour is a sort of parsley–caraway blend with a less strong aniseed flavour than fennel's. For the all-in-one gardener the fact that dill is an annual and runs to seed fairly quickly is both an advantage and a disadvantage: it can be allowed to self-seed prettily through sunny borders but it never produces a rich crop of leaves for fish dishes or seeds.

Fennel

This stout, vigorous, determinedly upright perennial has a notably aniseed flavour and the same thread-like foliage as dill but appearing year after year. Fennel makes wonderful fresh green (or purple) foaming mounds in spring; later its bold stems are topped with flat heads of tiny yellow flowers. Use sparingly in salads, as a garnish or on the barbecue with fish.

Graham's top tips for fennel

- CHOOSING VARIETIES There only two types: green-leaved *Foeniculum vulgare* and the especially useful purple/bronze-leaved *F. vulgare* 'Purpureum', a superb border plant.
- BUYING, SOWING AND PLANTING Buy plants, which are widely available, or sow seed in the open ground. Grow in any reasonable soil in full sun.
- CARE Dead-head after flowering to prevent a mass of self-sown seedlings. Fleshy roots do not divide easily, but there are usually plenty of seedlings to take the place of tired plants.
- HARVESTING Cut leaves at any time.
- GOOD COMPANIONS The purple variant is wonderful with white or scarlet tulips in spring, when its dense feathery mounds are at their most impressive, then later with pink linarias or achilleas or oriental poppies.

Fennel foliage is divided into delicate strands which makes a billowing, feathery mound early in the season and stretches taller as the season progresses.

Garlic chives

This invaluable member of the onion family produces flat green leaves with a mild garlic flavour and upright stems topped with slightly domed heads of white, starry, unexpectedly sweet-scented summer flowers. Its leavescan be used to add a gentle touch of garlic to salads. Grow this neat, attractive, front-of-the-border perennial in a sunny, fairly well-drained position with heucheras or among phygelius.

Hyssop

These twiggy little blue-flowered bushes with short, dark leaves make excellent informal hedges in the potager, and their flowers are tasty in salads. The leaves, with their strong, sage-like flavour, can also be used, but sparingly. More often available from herb specialists than in garden centres, the blue-flowered variant is the most often seen, yet there are also lovely white- and pink-flowered varieties. All three make an attractive mixed low hedge, or use them separately. Plant in any open, sunny place. As the flowers open, nip off shoot tips for culinary use; older leaves have a rather coarse flavour. Trim back hard in spring to keep plants bushy.

Lavender

Lavender is an unforgettable and invaluable herb, available in a rapidly increasing range of lovely varieties. These small woody shrubs have often greyish, slender or perhaps prettily divided, evergreen leaves. They are generally from sunny, dry habitats.

The increasing range of lavender varieties is ideal for sunny, well-drained situations and they look especially good when mulched with gravel.

Their scent is good in the house. In the kitchen they can be used sparingly in salads and marinades.

Graham's top tips for lavender

- CHOOSING VARIETIES There are basically two types: English lavender with its long, slender flower spikes in purple, lavender, pink or white; and French lavender with its shorter, fatter spikes topped by striking 'sails' in a similar colour range. These have long, slender leaves.

Some less common varieties produce prettily dissected leaves but are less hardy. An increasing range of attractive hybrids is now appearing, including variegated ones.

- BUYING, SOWING AND PLANTING Buy named varieties as plants from the garden centre or mail order specialist. Can be raised from seed but results are less good. Grow in a sunny site with good drainage.
- CARE Trim back specimens and hedges after flowering to about 2.5cm (1in) from old growth. Can be very long lived, especially if pruned regularly, but in very rich conditions plants may need replacing every four or five years.
- HARVESTING Pick flowers as they open and young leaves as they are needed.
- GOOD COMPANIONS Is excellent as a low hedge along a path and around a potager. Also useful as specimens in well-drained, Mediterranean gardens with other sun-lovers as well as in terracotta pots on sunny balconies or patios, close to nose level.

Lemon balm

Two yellow-leaved variants in particular are invaluable as easy, vigorous border perennials for dappled or partially shaded places and as delightfully lemony flavourings. Lemon balm is unremarkable in flower, but you can use the resting leaves in winter, as well as in spring and summer when in full growth.

The forms of lemon balm that have coloured foliage look good and grow well both in containers and borders but, unless the flowers are nipped off, they can become straggly.

Plants self-sow generously and the brightness of their yellow leaves often turns up in unexpected – as well as unsatisfactory – places. Lemon balm is a welcome addition to summer drinks and a pleasure to weed through as it gives off its lemony fragrance.

Graham's top tips for lemon balm

- CHOOSING VARIETIES 'Allgold' produces bright yellow leaves. For something less intense try 'Aureum', with leaves that are yellow at the centre and green at the edge.
- BUYING AND PLANTING Buy from a nursery and plant in any good soil in partial shade. In most climates the yellow leaves scorch in full sun especially if allowed to dry out. In full shade plants lose their colour.

- CARE Snip off flower stems to prevent self-seeding and to encourage fresh new foliage. Lift in early spring, divide and reduce in size if clumps become too large.
- HARVESTING Nip off shoots and leaves as needed; lemon balm tolerates regular picking.
- GOOD COMPANIONS Is excellent for brightening slightly shady corners among evergreen shrubs, hellebores and hardy geraniums, and in spring with daffodils, blue scillas or short red tulips.

Mint

The one herb that can be found in almost every British garden is mint, which is a useful and easy perennial for the all-in-one garden, especially in its coloured-leaved variants. It has a variety of kitchen uses, including teas, sauces, salads and summer drinks. Mint's one problem is that it tends to be invasive. The questing roots spread widely, especially in moist soil, creating dense clumps of upright stems with paired, highly aromatic leaves. Fortunately, the all-in-one gardener has an automatic solution: plant the pretty coloured foliage varieties, which are less invasive than plain green-leaved ones.

Graham's top tips for mint

- CHOOSING VARIETIES My top two for the all-in-one garden are ginger mint (*Mentha* x *gracilis* 'Variegata') with its yellow-veined leaves and variegated apple mint (*M. suaveolens* 'Variegata')

with its creamy leaf edges and the occasional all-cream shoot. Many other mints have bright or greyish leaves and attractive flower spikes.
- BUYING, SOWING AND PLANTING Buy plants from garden centres or mail order specialists. To minimize invasiveness, plant in a leaky bucket or large pot sunk in the ground with just the rim protruding. Grow in partial shade to full sun in good soil that does not dry out. Mints make good container plants but may overrun less robust companions.
- CARE Keep from drying out. Stand containers in a saucer in which you can leave water. Restrict vigorous forms if necessary.
- HARVESTING Pick shoots and leaves as needed.
- GOOD COMPANIONS Some mints may invade less resilient neighbours, but hostas and bergenias are sufficiently robust to coexist happily.

Oregano

This classic ingredient of Italian cooking, and other cuisines, is an easy, unexpectedly hardy perennial to grow. Its small, rounded, opposite leaves are clustered on twiggy stems, and it bears spikes of purple flowers. There are many golden-leaved and variegated varieties, features that alone justify a place in the all-in-one garden.

Graham's top tips for oregano

- CHOOSING VARIETIES Try: 'Aureum' (yellow leaves), 'Country Cream' (leaves with irregular cream or yellow edges), 'Gold Tip' (yellow tips to the leaves), 'Polyphant' (white-edged leaves and white flowers) or 'Thumble's Variety' (yellowish-green leaves with a milder flavour and white flowers). 'True Greek' has the most intense flavour but tends to be straggly or coarse. There are more.
- BUYING, SOWING AND PLANTING Buy plants from good garden centres and mail order specialists. Only the plain green-leaved variant is available from seed. Grow at the front of a sunny, well-drained border or one that is slightly shaded from the midday sun.
- CARE Vigorous, yellow-leaved and golden varieties may need some shade to prevent summer leaf scorch, especially in very dry conditions. Cut back after flowering and water well to encourage more leaves.
- HARVESTING Pick leaves and shoots as needed.
- GOOD COMPANIONS These ideal front-of-the-border plants for sites with a little shade are good around newly planted box hedging if not allowed to smother the new plants.

Both golden-leaved and variegated oreganos are excellent front of the border plants, especially early in the season, but nip off the flowers to keep them looking attractive.

Parsley

Parsley is one of the most valuable of herbs and indispensable to the all-in-one gardener. It has the foliage and habit to suit many garden situations, and it looks good with many other plants. This herb can be used in the kitchen both as a flavouring and as a garnish. Although flat-leaved parsley has the best flavour, curly varieties, with their leaves held tightly in attractive mounds, look so much better that they are a better choice for the all-in-one gardener.

Curly parsley is probably the one indispensable herb for all-in-one gardeners as it's invaluable in the kitchen and goes well with so many other plants.

Graham's top tips for parsley

- CHOOSING VARIETIES Almost all curly varieties are good, though 'Curlina' and 'Envy' have the Award of Garden Merit and 'Aphrodite' is reckoned to be especially good through winter. Garden centre plants may not be labelled with their variety name.
- BUYING, SOWING AND PLANTING Plants are often available in the garden centre, which is helpful as seed tends to germinate slowly and erratically. Soak seeds overnight in warm water to speed things up. Plant in spring or summer in containers, including hanging baskets, or in sun or partial shade in good fertile soil that neither dries out nor is waterlogged.
- CARE Parsley is a biennial that will eventually run to seed and can be allowed to self-sow.
- HARVESTING As required, pick the whole leaf, with its stalk, to keep plants looking neat. Modern curly varieties should last all season, and those planted late will be useful in winter.
- GOOD COMPANIONS Grow in window-boxes, containers or the front of borders with trailing tomatoes, yellow dwarf marigolds or white alyssum; also excellent as a temporary formal edging and to give structure to new plantings.

Rosemary

Rosemary has been long valued as a low evergreen informal hedge and as flavouring for lamb. This attractive shrub with its slim, dark green leaves and long season of small blue flowers is another herb that deserves its place in sunny situations – irrespective of its culinary value.

Graham's top tips for rosemary

- CHOOSING VARIETIES There are many varieties, including some with pink or white flowers, instead of the usual blue, and even with a trailing habit. 'Miss Jessopp's Upright' is good for hedges and an old favourite. 'Arp' is unusually hardy, with slightly lemon-flavoured leaves; 'Benenden Blue' is a trailer with pale blue flowers to cascade over low walls. 'Roseus' is pink. 'Severn Sea' is bushy and spreading in violet-blue, while 'Sissinghurst Blue' is upright, unusually hardy and very prolific in flower.
- BUYING, SOWING AND PLANTING Always buy plants of named varieties to be sure of the qualities you need. Can also be grown from seed, sown in spring. Plant in spring or summer in a sunny situation in soil that is fairly well drained. Thrives especially well in limey or chalky soil.
- CARE Rosemary is not good in very cold winters, especially if the soil is wet; the weight of snow may also damage branches. Tidy up and remove dead and straggly growth in spring, and shorten growth in summer after flowering to encourage bushiness.
- HARVESTING Nip off shoots, including flowering tops, as needed.
- GOOD COMPANIONS Thrives with other Mediterranean plants in sunny, well-drained conditions – sages, euphorbias and wild spring bulbs, for example – and makes a splendid container specimen and low hedge.

Sage

All-in-one gardeners are fortunate in that sage is another plant worth growing for its visual appeal alone but that also has good culinary value. These low

Purple sage is one of a number of varieties with unusually attractive foliage that thrive in containers as well as in beds and borders.

Mediterranean shrubs with their soft oval leaves produce attractive spikes of blue flowers in summer above front-of-the-border mounds of aromatic tactile foliage. A mix of different sage varieties, all clipped to the same height, makes an interesting edging.

Graham's top tips for sage

- CHOOSING VARIETIES For foliage colour try 'Aurea' (yellow leaves with green veins), 'Berggarten' (very broad leaves on compact plants), 'Icterina' (yellow-edged leaves), 'Kew Gold' (yellow leaves on neat plants), 'Purpurascens' (greyish-purple leaves) or 'Tricolor' (pink and cream markings; can be rather weak).
- SOWING AND PLANTING Buy plants from garden centres or mail order specialists to be sure of getting good varieties that have interesting leaves. Plant in any good soil in full sun in spring or summer.
- CARE Prune back after flowering, though do not cut into old wood, which may not regrow. After a few years plants tend to become too woody and open in the centre; replace them.
- HARVESTING Nip off leaves and young shoots as needed. This may well keep the plants bushy.
- GOOD COMPANIONS Plant in decorative ribbons, with rudbeckias and short nicotianas. Thrives in a sunny border, with blue veronica, perhaps. Also excellent as a specimen in a pot, among pots of scarlet or magenta celosia.

There are a vast variety of thymes available now with flowers in a range of colours and coloured foliage; all enjoy plenty of sunshine.

Thyme

There are many fine thymes. All are evergreen with tiny leaves and pretty summer flowers, which attract aphid-eating hoverflies. Some are rather bushy and provide the best shoots for the kitchen; others grow absolutely flat on the soil and flower more brilliantly but are of less culinary value. There are many varieties with colourful leaves (mainly in the bushier thymes) and with good flowers (predominantly in the creeping types).

Graham's top tips for thyme

- CHOOSING VARIETIES Lemon thyme (*Thymus* x *citriodorus*) is bushy, with lilac summer flowers.

Good variants include 'Golden King' (yellow-edged leaves) and 'Silver Queen' (silver-edged leaves and pink shoot tips in winter). Common thyme (*T. vulgaris*) is bushy, with usually purple flowers; try 'Silver Posie' (white-edged leaves and pink flowers). Broad-leaved thyme (*T. pulegioides*) is spreading in habit but bushy. Good variants include 'Archer's Gold' (yellow leaves) and 'Bertram Anderson' (red shoot tips and golden leaves). Among creeping thymes *T.* Coccineus Group bears magenta flowers and *T. serpyllum* 'Pink Chintz' has rose-pink flowers.

- BUYING, SOWING AND PLANTING Buy plants, so you can be sure of getting the correct variety; seed-raised plants do not have the foliage colour or the flowering impact of named varieties. Grow in sunny, well-drained conditions. Plant bushy types in gravel gardens, large troughs, alongside gravel paths and at the front of beds and borders. Creeping types will spread over gravel; they can also be set between paving stones, though they may become too hot unless shaded for a few hours a day in summer.
- CARE Trim bushy types back lightly after flowering to keep them well shaped. Prevent fallen leaves and neighbouring plants smothering growth. Pinch out all-green shoots from coloured-leaved variants.
- HARVESTING Pinch off shoots as needed; this in itself may keep plants bushy.

Borage is an easy and attractive annual herb whose seedlings appear in beds around the garden and even in gravel paths.

- GOOD COMPANIONS Creeping thymes are ideal when allowed to expand out from under frontal shrubs and are good cover for wild spring crocuses. They also spread out prettily over gravel on to paths. Bushy types are successful with creeping euphorbias or as specimens in terracotta pots.

The fragrance of chamomile foliage is always welcome and its flowers look delightful when set against its finely divided leaves.

Herbs round-up

Among other plants that are attractive and useful in the all-in-one garden is **angelica**, which is a bold and statuesque biennial for the back of the border. However, it is not a herb that many people actually use for anything; it does have some attractive, purple-tinted variants like 'Gigas'. **Bergamot**, in a wide variety of colourful flowering variants, is a fine border perennial and its aromatic flowers are good in teas. Annual **borage**, with its star-like, blue or more rarely white flowers is very pretty, although the flower-to-leaf ratio is a little low. The flowers and the cucumber-flavoured leaves are often used in summer drinks, and the flowers can be frozen individually in ice cubes.

The true **chamomile** comes in a non-flowering, groundcovering variant, while the wild variant with its little white daisies is valued for medicinal use. **Feverfew**, especially in its bright yellow-leaved forms, is a highly aromatic plant with white daisy flowers and is grown for its medicinal powers. As with all medicinal herbs, ask professional advice before actually using feverfew. **Horseradish** is a very tough, rather invasive, largely ineradicable perennial. Its variegated form is sometimes grown even though it may revert to plain green. **Perilla (shiso)** is a relative of coleus and basil with leaves that are used in Japanese cooking. It comes in green- and purple-leaved types, and the latter is sometimes used in summer bedding schemes. Perilla thrives in hot summers. **Tansy** is a vigorous and attractive, lacy leaved perennial, which is rather pungent and rarely used as a herb. It has a lovely, bright yellow-leaved form.

Edible flowers

Many flowers are edible and make decorative additions to salads. They are also useful as garnishes as well as in the garden.

Calendula

Sometimes known as English, or pot, marigold, calendulas bear orange, gold or yellow, often double, daisy flowers. The edible petals can be pulled from the flowers and scattered on salads. The whole plant has a characteristic attractive fragrance and varies in height from 23cm (9in) to 60cm (2ft) or more. These annuals are easy to raise from spring-sown seed and look great with purple fennel, blue borage or violas.

Daisy

Larger flowered, double forms of the familiar lawn daisy come in various red and pink shades, plus white, with some bicolours. While those with the largest flowers are a bit over the top, the neater, button-flowered varieties make excellent spring edging having been raised as biennials from summer-sown seed. Daisies are good as edging and for small beds and potagers.

Day lily

America's favourite perennial, with its fans of slender foliage and its large, lily-like flowers, is gaining in popularity worldwide. It comes in a spectacular range of colours and colour combinations. Dark colours are generally reckoned to be peppery in flavour, while the paler ones tend to taste rather sweet. The unopened flowerbuds can be deep fried or used in stir-fries and in cheesecake. Day lilies are ideal in mixed borders.

Geranium

Scented-leaved geraniums (frost-tender but vigorous summer plants) have aromatic foliage and small, mainly white or purplish flowers. They are less flamboyant than the more familiar geraniums of pots and bedding. Scented-leaved geraniums are also excellent in containers and in hot, sunny borders. They come with a range of mint- or citrus-flavoured leaves and their often prettily patterned or veined flowers are always useful in the kitchen.

Both the attractive marbled leaves of 'Alaska' nasturtiums and their colourful flowers are edible and often used in salads.

Nasturtium

The flowers, leaves and seeds of this vigorous bushy or climbing annual are all edible, and the flowers, mainly in fiery shades, are especially useful for brightening salads. The peppery leaves are just the right size to go in rolls or sandwiches. There are many decorative varieties such as the bushy 'Alaska', with its white-marbled leaves and flowers in up to ten different colours. It makes a fine container plant in tubs or baskets, a good edger tumbling over raised beds and a marvellous, one-season edging for new potagers. Nasturtiums grow too lush in rich conditions, so plant them around upright or step-over fruit trees, which will take up much of the water.

Pineapple guava

This impressive evergreen shrub produces grey-green leaves, felted in white on the undersides and, in summer, noticeably fleshy red and white flowers, which can be eaten straight from the tree. Pineapple guava is not the hardiest of shrubs, so grow it against a hot and sunny wall. It is also good in containers if they can be protected over the winter.

Sunflower

These familiar annual flowers are easy to grow and cheerfully coloured. Sunflowers are available in an increasing range of heights (45–3m/1½–10ft), colours (from creamy white through every shade of yellow to orange and mahogany) and flower sizes (5–30cm/ 2–12in). Seeds, buds and petals are all edible, although you might find the buds of the largest flowers uncomfortably chewy.

Tulbaghia

Tulbaghia is a rarely seen and rather tender member of the onion family. It has pretty lilac flowers, with a mild, chives-like flavour, held on open heads over spreading slender foliage. In some varieties the leaves are striped in cream. Grow as a specimen for containers and give a little shelter in winter. Tulbaghia is very attractive as it matures and fills its pot.

Viola

In a vast range of flower sizes and patterns, violas are one of the few flowers to include every colour of the spectrum – plus black and white. Different varieties can be in flower all the year round, except in very hot climates. For the all-in-one garden use seed-raised violas as they are neat and prolific and make a lovely edible garnish. They are especially useful in containers and as edging plants.

05 | Planting and Maintenance

Much of the success of the all-in-one garden is the result of proper preparation. No, this doesn't mean hours of back-breaking digging and moving endless barrowloads of steaming manure, though that is fine and will give great results, if you like the exercise. It is more a case of providing plants with a good start and then giving them a little attention now and again when they need it.

Good soil really does make a difference. But rather than striving for some mystical ideal, a far more realistic plan is to give plants the conditions they appreciate and improve bad soil in a way that suits the plants you wish to cultivate.

Of course, at times, plants will have problems, but growing them in suitable conditions is the best way to prevent poor growth and attack by pests and diseases. A plant that is thriving is less likely to succumb to infestation and infection.

Planting a standard bay tree allows plenty of light underneath in which to grow a bright tapestry of kale, chard, nasturtiums and marigolds.

Soil preparation

Getting soil ready for planting is important but it need not be too exhaustive; even just a little thoughtful preparation can make a big difference to conditions.

New planting areas

Digging or forking is necessary in gardens or beds that are being created for the first time or where there was previously lawn. The soil needs to be loosened to at least the depth of the spade blade or fork tines; if you're feeling fit and enthusiastic, preparing soil to twice the depth of the spade blade is ideal. At the same time it is important to add organic matter, because all-in-one gardens tend to be densely planted. Plants absorb a great deal of moisture and nutrients, both of which are provided by organic matter.

Break up the ground with a digging fork or spade – not with a so-called border fork (or lady's fork), which is shorter. The best all-round approach is to mark out the new planting area, then fork or dig it over thoroughly in a systematic manner; work across the plot in rows, moving backwards row by row. When you have finished, spread 7.5–10cm (3–4in) of organic matter (*see* page 162) over the whole surface and then go over the plot again, working it in with your fork. Finally, firm the whole bed by shuffling across the plot in tight, side-by-side steps. Rake level, add some general balanced fertilizer – organic or not as you prefer (check the pack for rates) – then rake it in and you are then ready to start planting.

Adding to existing plantings

Whenever your lettuce is harvested or the beans finally fizzle out, you need to do more than simply look at the tattered remains of the crop. First, remove the debris to the compost heap. Then, if the space is very small, work over the soil with a trowel or hand fork, add in some fine, weed-free garden compost or old potting compost and then you are ready to plant again. If a whole group of plants occupying a larger space has been removed, take the same approach but use a border fork.

Often you may want to slip a few young plants in among mature plants that are already in place – some annuals in under the currants, perhaps. Use a trowel to scrape away the soil very carefully so as not to damage existing roots when you make the hole.

Raised beds

Digging to twice the depth of the spade blade is sometimes recommended and is certainly the best approach as it allows roots to penetrate deeply into improved soil, but it is also hard work – the spirit may be willing but the flesh less so. Forking over to the full depth of a digging fork's tines, spreading 7.5–10cm (3–4in) of well-rotted garden compost or other weed-free organic matter on the top and then working it in with the fork is the most practical approach for most people. On a larger scale, the same result can be achieved with a powerful rotary tiller. Then shuffle all over the area to remove any air pockets. Cropping in raised beds is very intense, so fork over or dig it well every three years, working in a 5cm (2in) mulch at some convenient point in the planting cycle.

Compost and mulch

Organic matter is marvellous. It has the wonderful capacity to improve both sandy soil and clay soil; it holds plant foods and releases them steadily; and it also retains moisture. When spread on the soil surface it conserves moisture and prevents weed growth.

Organic matter comes, for example, as bagged soil improver from garden centres, as garden compost, as bagged manure bought from stables and farms, and as used potting compost from your tubs and hanging baskets. However, it must be weed free – what a waste to spread a neat mulch of compost to help suppress weeds only to see the mulch itself sprout a crop.

Bagged soil improver is virtually guaranteed to be weed free. At the opposite end of the price range, your own used potting compost may also be weed-free, although old seed compost may sprout seeds that failed to come up when you first sowed them. Both bagged soil improver and used potting compost have the advantage of a fine, crumbly texture, which is ideal when they are spread as a mulch, 5–7.5cm (2–3in) deep, on soil after planting to retain moisture and prevent weed growth. The mulch can be worked in when the crop is first removed and before planting again. Such crumbly textured matter is also suitable for working into soil when preparing for planting.

Manure may sprout unexpected seedlings, like barley perhaps, and garden compost may also be full of weed seeds. These are best buried under fruit bushes and perennials when planting. They can rest undisturbed, providing nutrients to long-term plants.

My warning about garden compost, however, should not deter you from using weeds, vegetable and other plant debris and even lawn mowings in your own compost heap. The key to good compost is to build a timber bin, which provides good insulation, and to add some garden soil to provide the bacteria that get the process off to a flying start. As the heap starts to rot it heats up – and the hotter the heap the more weed seeds will be killed.

All vegetable debris and weeds without invasive roots can go on the compost heap; the hotter it gets while rotting, the more useful the compost will be.

Watering

Food plants are largely made up of water, so the availability of sufficient moisture in the soil can make all the difference between a good crop and a poor one, a fleeting crop and a long-season one.

Climates are changing worldwide; some regions are becoming wetter and others drier, but in most gardens there are times in the growing season when rain just does not come. So watering is important. The question is how to give plants the water they need with as little waste as possible.

First of all, collect rainwater from the greenhouse, conservatory, garage or house roof and store it in water butts. This is perfect for watering plants but should never be used for seeds or young seedlings, because rainwater usually contains fungi, which may harm them. Some gardeners direct run-off from roofs into a pond, so do not use that for seedlings either.

Although you may have many water butts, mains water is going to be your usual source. Use it wisely. For containers, use a watering can or install a drip system, perhaps on a timer, which applies water exactly where and when it is needed.

On beds and borders a seep hose (also known as leaky pipe or porous pipe) is the only answer. This rubber pipe, often made from recycled car tyres, is perforated with tiny holes so the water steadily seeps out. Run it, evenly spaced, over the bed, then spread the mulch to hide it. When you turn on the tap, all the water goes directly into the soil. Brilliant.

Never water plants by connecting a sprinkler to one end of a hose and a tap to the other, then turning on the tap and forgetting about it. A sprinkler is the most inefficient way of watering, as most of the water evaporates before it even reaches the plant roots.

The most efficient way to water, which wastes almost no water at all, is to use a seep hose which drips steadily to soak the soil slowly.

Seed sowing

Most of the all-in-one garden plants that are raised regularly and repeatedly are raised from seed. The range of plants suitable for this approach is wide, so it is advisable to rely primarily on the advice given on the seed packet, which is tuned to the needs of each individual crop or even each variety. The following, therefore, are but guidelines.

Sowing seeds in pots

To avoid the sight of more soil than plants in the all-in-one garden, most plants should be raised from seed in pots or plug trays and then planted out when relatively mature. Choose pots rather than seed trays for sowing seed, unless you need a very large number of plants. New or thoroughly washed, plastic pots,

In most cases a pot will be large enough to take all the seeds you need to sow; using a seed tray wastes space and will encourage you to sow too many plants.

7.5cm (3in) or 9cm (3½in) across, are ideal. Square pots take up less space than round ones. Always choose fresh seed compost from the garden centre. Never use potting or seed compost that has been previously used or garden soil, which carries the risk of disease.

Fill each pot loosely with moist seed compost. Remove any surplus to leave it level with the top of the pot. Tap the pot on the table or bench a few times to settle the compost, then press gently with the bottom of another pot to remove any air pockets. Sow the seeds thinly, then cover with a little compost. The seed packet will give details that are more directly related to its contents.

Water the compost gently with a fine rose on the watering can. Then cover with a sheet of glass, clear plastic or place the pot in a clear polythene bag. Stand the pot in a propagator, on the window-sill or greenhouse bench or in a sheltered corner outside, depending on the seed.

Once seedlings are developing their first true leaf (one that looks like a miniature version of a mature leaf), they can be moved to individual pots or plugs of their own. They are then grown on and planted out at a size when they make an instant impression.

Sowing seeds in plug trays

Many vegetables and herbs are best raised in plug trays. These usually come as 20 or 24 individual 2.5cm (1in) cells attached loosely to one another, though there is a vast range of sizes and formats. Such trays are often rather flimsy but can generally be used a few times if washed carefully.

Fill a clean plug tray with fresh seed compost, scrape off the surplus and level off using fingers or the base of another tray. Using the point of an old pencil or slender cane, make a slight depression in the centre of each cell and sow two to four seeds, as necessary, in each, then move a little compost across to cover them. Water, cover with glass or plastic, then place in a propagator, on a window-sill or greenhouse bench, or in a sheltered place outside. When the seedlings appear, thin to one if necessary or leave all to develop. Gradually accustom seedlings to garden conditions, then plant them out.

Sowing seeds outside

In a few situations, especially in raised beds, sowing seeds directly into the soil outside is an option. Rake moist soil to a fine texture and remove stones and weed seeds. Lay the rake across the bed and use it as a guide to draw a line (a drill) in the soil with the point of a cane or even your finger. Check the seed packet for the depth required. If the soil is dry, water along the drill with a watering can. Sprinkle the seeds thinly in the drill; 1–2cm (½–¾in) apart is usually about right. Then use fingers or the back of the rake to bring a little soil from the sides to cover the seeds. Firm the soil gently with your palm or the back of the rake.

When the seedlings emerge they may need thinning out (*see* page 168). Check the seed packet.

Planting

The best planting technique varies slightly depending on the plant type: small short-term plants; perennials; trees, shrubs or fruit bushes.

Annuals and short-term vegetables

Relatively small, short-term plants should be set out in plugs or from pots. If the soil has not been improved recently, work in the mulch with a hand fork together with a handful of general fertilizer to the square metre (yard). Water the plants with a liquid feed an hour or so before planting. Set out the plants, in their pots, or remove them from their plug tray and set them out, adjusting their positions and spacing as required. Then remove each plant from its pot (if appropriate). With a trowel make a hole just a little bigger than the plant's

rootball, slip it in, fill any gaps with soil and firm gently with the fingers. The top of the rootball should be at, or a little below, the soil level. When all is done, water in with more liquid feed, then mulch.

Perennials

Ornamental perennials and perennial vegetables like rhubarb may be in their positions for many years, so more thorough soil preparation is required. Otherwise the planting technique is generally the same as for annuals. If the soil has been well prepared, the only further task will be to work in old mulch. If not, it pays to fork some organic matter and a handful of fertilizer into the bottom of the hole before planting. Some perennials are sold as large plants, so a spade may be

RIGHT: *Prepare well for planting larger plants by making a good sized hole and working in plenty of organic matter to give the plants a good start.*

LEFT: *Small but well-developed plants can be slipped in easily amongst established plants, or planted in rows or patches, and will make an immediate impact.*

needed as well as a garden fork to loosen the soil at the bottom of the hole. Water the plants with a liquid feed before and after planting, then mulch well.

Trees, shrubs and fruit bushes

Irrespective of any recent general soil improvements, dig a hole at least half as wide again as the rootball of the tree, shrub or fruit bush. Fork over the base of the hole thoroughly. Remove some of the soil and replace with organic matter and a handful of fertilizer. Fork this in. Firm the base of the hole with the ball of your foot and check its depth while the plant is still in its pot: the top of the rootball should be level or a little below the surrounding soil.

Water the plant with a liquid feed, then remove it from its pot. Orientate it in the hole so that its best-furnished and most even side faces the front. Work more organic matter and another handful of fertilizer into the first soil you dug from the planting hole. Backfill around the rootball with this improved soil and firm with your hands or the ball of your foot. Water with a liquid feed again after planting, then mulch the surface well.

Some fruit bushes, especially raspberries, are not supplied in pots but are sold with their roots bare, having been dug up from the nursery shortly before sale. Often the bare roots are dry, so they should be soaked overnight in water (better still with some seaweed fertilizer added) before planting.

Keeping control

Plant and forget? No thank you. Plants in the all-in-one garden need attention to ensure they give their best, both in the early days and more regularly on a long-term basis.

Thinning seedlings

In some cases seedlings sown in the open garden need thinning to allow them sufficient space to develop properly. Check the seed packet for spacing requirements. Water the rows first if the soil is not moist, then place two protective fingers from one hand on either side of the seedling you wish to keep and pull out those around it. In many cases it pays to thin in two stages: first to one-half or one-third spacing, then to final spacing. This provides a solution if any seedlings die or are damaged – they can be replaced with one of those that would otherwise be removed.

Transplanting

Seedlings raised in the open ground are best started in a quiet corner (*see* pages 165 and 170), then transplanted. They are usually thinned once. Then, as they increase in size, the young plants are watered and carefully lifted from the soil using a trowel, keeping as much soil on the roots as possible, and planted in their permanent sites, where they are watered in with a liquid feed.

Pinching

Many bushy plants need the tips of their shoots pinched out occasionally. This helps herb plants to

RIGHT: *Small perennial plants can often be simply dug up in spring and pulled apart by hand before being replanted in improved soil.*

LEFT: *Fruits vary in the type of pruning required, often this is outlined on the label or you can consult a specialized pruning book.*

keep well branched and to produce more useful green shoots. With thumb and forefinger, pinch out growing tips in the early stages to encourage bushiness in annual flowers. Pinching out also prevents plants running to seed, which usually shortens their life; and it can also be a useful way of dealing with the beginnings of mildew on shoot tips.

Dividing plants

Perennial plants, be they ornamentals such as hardy geraniums, herbs like oregano or vegetables like globe artichokes, are best divided every few years to keep them vigorous and prevent them becoming congested. This can be done in autumn or spring. Dig up the plant, shake off some of the soil. Discard old and woody material from the centre of the clump, then split the remaining younger growth, from the edges, into smaller pieces. Improve the soil (*see* page 162) and then replant.

Pruning

Pruning trees and shrubs grown both for their fruit and ornamental features makes a significant contribution to their productivity and visual appeal. It can also keep them to the required size. Always use good-quality secateurs and a pruning saw when occasionally necessary – a bread knife and a rusty carpenter's saw from the back of the shed are not adequate substitutes. Always cut to just above a bud. Brief pruning suggestions are given under the appropriate plant entries (*see* pages 102–115).

Succession

There are three ways of ensuring that as little bare soil as possible is on view as a succession of crops and flowers approach maturity: by sowing and transplanting; by sowing in pots or plug trays, then planting out; or by buying young plants.

Except in the case of cut-and-come-again crops, sowing where plants are to mature results in a sparse display while the plants germinate and begin to fill out. To avoid this, sow seed in a small, dedicated, out-of-the-way corner that is not too shady and then transplant the seedlings. Sowing and transplanting often works well, although it is not ideal for all crops and not all gardens can provide a suitable site.

Sow seed in a short row, perhaps less than 50cm (20in) long. As the seedlings grow, thin them out and, when they are large enough, move them into their final site. In some cases you may need only six plants to set out, so this process is not too demanding of space.

If you prefer, sow seed in pots and transplant the seedlings into plug trays or grow on individually in pots. They can also be sown directly in plug trays and the plugs planted out or moved into a pot to develop before planting out at a larger size.

The third option is to take advantage of the growing number of catalogues that list young plants of vegetables and herbs grown by specialist nurseries in plugs. You can sometimes plant the plugs straight in the ground; other plugs need to be planted in pots and grown on for a few weeks to allow them to develop more fully. And by growing on these plug plants in pots they will usually make an worthwhile impact from the day they are planted.

LEFT: *Raising young plants in modules rather than in the garden where they are to mature allows you to make more use of space and leave less bare soil.*

To spray or not to spray

To a greater or lesser extent, everyone is wary of pesticides and fungicides, especially when used on food plants. The food in the supermarket, unless specifically labelled organic, will have been treated with chemicals to keep it pest- and disease-free and to kill weeds, and the products available to farmers and commercial growers are far more potent than those sold in garden centres to home gardeners. So even if you spray your all-in-one garden regularly, the treatments you use are likely to be less dangerous to yourself and your family and to the environment generally than those used on bought food.

Having said that, one of the advantages of the all-in-one approach is that crops are not grown in the traditional vegetable garden monocultures, which tend to attract pests and disease problems. Siting vegetables among other plants helps prevent pests actually finding the crops they feed on and minimizes their spread, because flowers and other ornamentals act as barriers.

But sometimes plants do succumb, and then what should you do? Picking off pests by hand can work for some of them, as can giving them a blast of soapy water from a sprayer. Diseased leaves can also be picked off. Various physical deterrents can be effective, too. Try sticky bands on fruit trees to prevent creatures climbing up to lay their eggs; or putting sharp gravel on top of the compost in containers to deter slugs.

There are also some very safe natural sprays to consider. The results may not be as dramatic as will be evident from the latest products of the laboratory, and plants may need treating more often. However, they do work.

There are also plant varieties that have resistance to pests and diseases built in by the breeder (and not by using genetic modification techniques). These should be especially sought out by the all-in-one gardener. They are often marked in seed catalogues and on seed packets. If the plants themselves ignore pests and diseases, is not that just ideal?

Graham's top tips on pest practicalities

- Choose pest- and disease-resistant varieties.
- Consider natural sprays and mild soapy water as treatments.
- Deter slugs with a sharp gravel mulch.
- Pick off by hand leaves carrying pests or diseases .
- Use sticky bands on fruit trees.
- Remember that the all-in-one approach itself helps reduce pest and disease problems.

Index

Acknowledgements

Joy Larkcom was an inspiration to my father in his vegetable growing and for many years has also been to me. Her intensely practical book, *Grow Your Own Vegetables*, should be on the bookshelf, and in the shed, of every vegetable grower – be you an all-in-one gardener or more traditional in your approach. Other inspiring gardeners and garden writers have used flowers and food plants together in creative and practical ways from Brian Halliwell, who planned the displays at Kew over thirty years ago, to Rosemary Verey at Barnsley House in Gloucestershire and, in the United States, Ros Creasey. They, thoughtful gardeners everywhere, and the plant breeders who have created so many varieties which are attractive as well as tasty and nutritious have all brought us to the point where it is indeed possible to create an All-in-One Garden.

My friends at Cassell Illustrated, Anna Cheifetz and Robin Douglas-Withers, have seen the book from conception to bound copy with impressive professionalism and good humour while my invaluable agent Vivien Green has cheerfully kept us all on our toes. Finally, as always, I thank my wife judy without whom neither this book, nor anything else, would be possible.

Graham Rice
Northamptonshire, April 2006

Picture Credits

Alamy/Geoff Kidd 119; /Trevor Sims 132; **Andrea Jones**/Garden Exposures Photo Library 12, 54 right, 163; **Garden Picture Library**/Mark Bolton 89; /David Cavagnaro 20; /Eric Crichton 52; /Macduff Everton 14; /Lynn Keddie 38, 50; /Michele Lamontagne 114; /Jane Legate 162; /judywhite, Design: Peter London 80; /Brenner Marion 49 left, 77; /Mayer/Le Scanff 87, 100; /Zara Mccalmont (Napier) 161; /Productions - Burke/Triolo 166; /Howard Rice 75 left; /Friedrich Strauss 72; /Mel Watson 145; /Jo Whitworth 130; **The Garden Collection**/Liz Eddison 93, 142, 156, /Design: Julian Dowle, RHS Chelsea 2005 126, /Design: Women's Institute with RHS Tatton Park 2005 19/Design: Georgina Steeds 49 right; /Andrew Lawson 95; /Derek St. Romaine 112, 136/Chateau de la Bourdaisiere 137; **GardenPhotos.com**/Graham Rice 2, 53, 84, 98, 127; /judywhite 10, 11 centre, 16, 17, 18, 27 top, 29 left, 29 right, 32, 35, 44, 63, 69, 75 right, 113, 125, 128, 138, 141, 150, 159 right, 167, /Design: Peter London 82; **GardenWorld Images** 121; **John Glover** 59, 106, 107, 109, 135, 159 centre, 164, /RHS Chelsea, Design: Rupert Golby 11 left, 21, 43; **Octopus Publishing Group Limited** 146; /Mark Bolton, Design: Alitex The Glasshouse Company, RHS Chelsea 2001 74, /Design: Carol Nottage, RHS Chelsea 2001 76; /Michael Boys 101 left, 108, 149, 154; /Jerry Harpur 140; /Marcus Harpur 159 left, 160; /Howard Rice 116, 122, 129, 168, 169; /Stephen Robson 7, 118, 157; George Wright 103, 105, 123, 134, 139; **Harpur Garden Library** 144; **Jerry Harpur** 29 centre, 31, 41, 41 bottom, 46; /RHS Chelsea, Design: Rupert Golby, 1995 9; /RHS Chelsea, Design: Bunny Guiness 54 left; /Design: Raymond Hudson 61; /Benington Lordship 96; /Design: Jeff Mendoza 62; /Dan Pearson 91; **Marcus Harpur** 101 centre, 117; /Old Rectory, Sudborough 153; /RHS Chelsea, Design: Geoff Whiten 56; **Andrew Lawson** 37, 60, 66, 102, 115, 147, 151; /Torie Chugg 27 bottom; **Marianne Majerus** 28, 158; **Clive Nichols**/Arrow Cottage Garden, Hereford 97, /Robert Clark 67 left, 70, /Design: Nigel Colborn 67 centre, 79, /Design: Sir Terence Conran 124, /Greencombe Garden, Somerset 99, /Hedens Lustgard, Sweden 64, /Simon Irvine 23, 57, /National Asthma, RHS Chelsea 1993 148, /Netherfield Herb Garden 42, /Jane Nichols 133, /Joe Swift 152; **Photolibrary Group**/MaXx Images 111; /Peter Rees 155; /Konrad Wothe 143; **Science Photo Library**/Mrs. W. D. Monks 110; **Jo Whitworth** 11 right, 25, 170, /RHS Hampton Court, Design: Karen Maskell 24, /RHS Gardens, Wisley, Surrey 104, /West Dean Gardens, W. Sussex 85

Planting plans on pages 33, 39. 45. 47 and 55 by Debbie Ryder.